Poet's England ~

Lancashire

**Compiled and illustrated
by
Gladys Mary Coles**

HEADLAND

First published in 1995
by
HEADLAND PUBLICATIONS
38 York Avenue, West Kirby
Wirral, Merseyside L48 3JF

© The authors, 1995

A full CIP record for this book is available
from the British Library

ISBN 0 903074 91 5

Headland gratefully acknowledges financial
assistance from North West Arts Board

Printed in Great Britain
by Bemrose Shafron (Printers) Ltd
Chester

FOREWORD

This was a challenging project - to compile an anthology of poems about Lancashire, evoking as many aspects of its life, places and people, as possible. I was aiming, especially, to show Lancashire's immense variety, its surprises, and, spanning five centuries, the extraordinary transformations it has undergone.

There are indeed few areas of Britain as widely various in their features and customs. Lancashire's landscape contrasts are dramatic - from the beauty of Pennine fells, moors and forests, to the coast, with resorts such as Blackpool; from villages, rivers and ports to areas of dense population, the industrial towns and vast conurbations of modern cities. Bounded along its entire western edge by the Irish Sea, Lancashire once included part of the Lake District and, stretching across the North West, took in Manchester and Liverpool. The drastic 1974 boundary changes left the county truncated and modern progress has seen its bisection by the M6. But Lancashire's character survives, transcending boundaries; and it offers far more than a speedy route to Cumbria and Scotland, as I hope this anthology demonstrates.

Here is a county strong in identity, noted for its humour and friendliness, yet not lacking in myths, legends and superstitions, in lively 'boggarts' and witches (associated with Pendle in particular). And it is rich in castles, abbeys, manors and churches. From the invasion of the Romans to the ravages of the Industrial Revolution, Lancashire and its people have lived through remarkable changes. The historic County Palatine, seat of the Dukes of Lancaster (one becoming King, as Henry IV), has been the scene of great events, of Jacobite, Civil War and Luddite struggles; and during the Industrial Age this region provided the foundation of Britain's power. Today, in an age of new technologies, the remaining mills are heritage sites.

In capturing Lancashire's essence and conveying its fascinating diversity, I have drawn mainly on the work of contemporary poets, the famous and the lesser-known, from both within the county and outside it. But also represented here are poets from the past, major figures such as Wordsworth, and (in extracts) the fathers of dialect poetry, of which there is a strong tradition in Lancashire. In my search for poems about specific places and facets, I had the opportunity, when tutoring creative writing courses, to engage the talents of local poets - and the work they produced now enhances the anthology. This reflects too the growth and vigour of writing activity in the North West today, and the stimulus given by the well-established Lancaster Literature Festival. I have enjoyed enormously the task of creating this composite portrait and I express my warm thanks to all who have helped.

May 1995   *Gladys Mary Coles*

LANCASHIRE: Map showing main places mentioned in the text

CONTENTS

Call of the North	Phoebe Hesketh	9
The Billmen of Bowland	Anon	10
Flodden Field	Anon	10
Lancashire	John Critchley Prince	11
Lancashire Fare	Jean Stanbury	11
Poly-Olbion	Michael Drayton	12
Lancashire	Michael May	12
An Awkward Journey	Tony MacDermott	13
Pennine Towns	John Ward	14
Pennines	John Cassidy	15
Snow from the North	Graham Mort	16
Martin Mere, in Late November	Alan Doherty	17
Southport by Night	Frances Nagle	18
At Formby	Andrew Young	18
Ormskirk Borders	Will Daunt	19
East Lancashire Road, A580	Gladys Mary Coles	20
Old Rhyme	Trad	20
Liverpool	George Perry	21
Liverpool 1777/Slaves	William Roscoe	21
Cotton Rhymes	Anon	22
A Masque of Liverpool	John Masefield	22
The Coming in of Ancestors	Gladys Mary Coles	23
Liverpool 8, 1942	Betty Jones	24
Directions	Matt Simpson	24
High Windows	Brian Wake	25
Liverpool	Roger McGough	26
In my Liverpool Home	Peter McGovern	26
Coda to The Civil War	John Calvert	27
Cat I' Th' Window	Margaret Ross	27
The Rainhill Trials	Sue Gerrard	28
Red Blood River	Albert Morgan	29
Winwick Church/Warrington Ale	Anon	30
Bewsey	John Fitchett	30
The Colliery Explosion, Haydock	Anon	31
TheWindle Witch	Sue Gerrard	32
Boggarts Abound	Carole Baldock	33
Pennington Flash	Sheila Clift	34
Over Billinge Lump	Albert Morgan	35
Our Only Father and Son Outing	Peter Street	36
The Way We Were in 1900	Angela Topping	37
Lancashire Textile Poem	Daphne Schiller	38
Pit Brow Lassies, Atherton 1918	John Calvert	38
A Lancashire Haiku	Lance Cleary	38
The Lamplighters	W.A. Mellors	39

v

Salford's Mining Museum	Eileen Holroyd	39
Walking Day	Deidre Armes Smith	40
Stretford	Gerald England	41
Old Trafford	Francis Thompson	41
Manchester to Bolton	John Ashbrook	41
The Peterloo Meeting	Anon	42
Two Millers	John Byrom	43
The Scenes of Manchester	Anon	43
Manchester Ship Canal	R.S.K.	43
Valette in Manchester	John Ward	44
Ben Brierley	Arthur Chappell	44
Home Town (Ashton-under-Lyne)	Mary Brett	45
The Irk	J. David Mallinson	46
Oldham: December	Gerald England	47
Newton Silk Mill (1832)	J. David Mallinson	48
Going to Shaw on the Train	Adele Geras	49
Millstone Grit	Wendy Bardsley	49
John Collier's Grave	Kathleen Johnston	50
Postcard Home to Rochdale	Ken Craven	50
Old Lancashire Riddle	Anon	51
Lancashire Hobby Horse	Carole Baldock	51
Bolton-Le-Moors, 1960	Phoebe Hesketh	52
Moorland Mill, near Bolton	Margaret Woodcock	52
Rivington Pike, Good Friday	Bessie Hall	53
Rivington Church	Rev. Jackson	54
November Day on Winter Hill	Barbara Horrocks	54
Etchings of Lambstop	Deirdre Woodcock	55
The Irwell Forge Band on Holcombe Hill	Chris Woods	56
Holcombe Poem	Adrian Henri	56
Rossendale	Anon	57
Rossendale	Brian Mitchell	57
Valley of the Kings	Patricia Foster	58
On These Hills	Martyn Halsall	59
Oh, The Wild, Wild Moors	Edwin Waugh	60
Come Whoam to thy Childer an' Me	Edwin Waugh	60
Waugh's Well	Chris Woods	61
On the Blackburn Road to Bolton	Antoinette Loftus	62
Come, Mary, link thi' Arm i' Mine	Edwin Waugh	62
Cutt Wood, Rishton	Valerie J. Calderwood	63
Hoghton Tower	Alison Chisholm	64
Bamber Bridge	Michael May	65
Place Rhyme	Trad	66
Iter Lancastrense	Richard James	66
A Lancashire Witch	Mike Pattinson	67
The Gymnasts	Phoebe Hesketh	68

The Foulridge Blacksmith's Epitaph	Anon	69
A Builder's Epitaph	Jack Whitaker	69
Welcome, Bonny Brid	Samuel Laycock	69
The Road to Chingle Hall	Norah Mortimer	70
Chingle Hall	Norah Mortimer	71
Place Rhymes	Trad	72
In Search of the Ribble	Marie Murray	72
The Trough of Bowland	Pauline Keith	73
Barn in Bowland	Sara Monk	74
Peter Lad	Averil King-Wilkinson	75
Ribblesdale	Gerard Manley Hopkins	76
Stone Dicta	Lauraine Palmeri	77
Day Saver to Preston	Patricia Pogson	78
Place Rhyme	Trad	78
The Ballad of Preston Dock	Ted Harris	79
Ribble Estuary	Betty Jones	80
Like Winter in Delhi (Lytham)	Seetha Shearer	81
Lytham St. Annes	Mike Read	82
The Fylde	Allen Clarke	82
First Sighting	C.M. Coates	83
The Pleasure Beach	Ceri Courtenay	84
Blackpool (In the Season)	Sheila Clift	84
Landau Driver	Nancy Clare Wynne	85
Last Night	Peggy Poole	86
Blackpool Wind	Sheila Clift	87
Dancing in the Dark - Blackpool	Michael Cunningham	87
The View from the Gallery	Jennifer Smethurst	88
Bleak Wyre	Roger Chamberlain	88
Sunderland Point (Sambo)	James Watson	89
Sunderland Point & Ribchester (an extract)	U.A. Fanthorpe	89
View from the Lune Aqueduct	Averil King-Wilkinson	90
Seeing through Lancaster Castle	Joyce Knowles	91
S. Martin's College, Lancaster	U.A. Fanthorpe	92
Time for Bed	Anne Spillard	93
The Promenade, Morecambe	Geoffrey Holloway	94
Morecambe Bay	Graham Mort	95
Night Shrimping	Mike Cooper	96
Strange Image at Warton Crag	Cynthia Kitchen	97
Cave Revisited, Silverdale 1990	Alan Gaunt	98
New Year's Eve 1913, Cartmel	Gordon Bottomley	99
The Levens Estuary	William Wordsworth	100
The Tower on the Hoad, Ulverston	H.D. Rawnsley	101
St. Cuthbert's Church, Aldingham	Anon	101
Furness Abbey	Mary Coleridge	102
Under the Horizon (Barrow)	Robert Drake	103

On Duddon Marsh	Norman Nicholson	104
Black Combe	Branwell Bronte	104
The Charcoal Burners	Irvine Hunt	105
The Veterans (an extract)	David Craig	106
Climbing for Birds'-Eggs	William Wordsworth	106
The Thunderstorm	Andrew Young	107
Coniston Water	John Ruskin	108
Ruskin at Rest	H.D. Rawnsley	109
To Hawkshead	William Wordsworth	109
Carol	John Short	110
Skating on Esthwaite Water	William Wordsworth	110
Dear Native Regions	William Wordsworth	111
Index of Poets		112

ACKNOWLEDGEMENTS

For the use of copyright material grateful acknowledgement is made to:
Faber and Faber Ltd and the Estate of Norman Nicholson for 'On Duddon Marsh' from *The Pot Geranium*. U.A. Fanthorpe and Peterloo Poets for 'S. Martins College, Lancaster' and an extract from 'Sunderland Point and Ribchester' from *A Watching Brief*. The Society of Authors for the Estate of John Masefield for an extract from *A Masque of Liverpool*. The Estate of Andrew Young for 'At Formby' and 'The Thunderstorm' from *Collected Poems of Andrew Young*.

David Craig and Secker and Warburg for an extract from 'The Veterans' and a quotation from *Native Stones*. Graham Mort and Dangaroo Press for 'Snow from the North' from *Snow from the North*; and 'Morecambe Bay' from *Sky Burial*. Duckworth & Co Ltd for Gladys Mary Coles' 'East Lancashire Road, A580' from *The Glass Island*; and 'The Coming in of Ancestors' from *Liverpool Folio*. Roger McGough for 'Liverpool' from *The Liverpool Scene* (ed. Edward Lucie-Smith); Adrian Henri and Penguin Books for 'Holcombe Poem' from *Penguin Modern Poets, Vol.10*.

For kind permission to include poems from their individual collections:
Phoebe Hesketh, Chris Woods, John Ashbrook, John Ward, Adèle Geras, John Cassidy, Alison Chisholm, Matt Simpson, Michael Cunningham, Mike Cooper, Brian Wake, Peter Street, Mike Read, Peggy Poole, J.D. Mallinson.

Special thanks are due to all the poets who have provided previously published and/or new work for the anthology; and to Guy Stapleton for some rare source material. Every effort has been made to trace and contact copyright holders; any omissions will be rectified on notification. Copyright remains with the authors; poems are dated by the first year of publication (where known).

CALL OF THE NORTH

We rebuilt our childhood, leaf by leaf,
that bright day snatched from summers half-forgotten
half-remembered -
the Brock running brown under bridges,
the badger at home
and a dipper with golf-ball breast
bobbing on glistening stone.

We followed the river
up lost paths, over gates and stiles
broken by the years,
past the farm whose cherry in spring
was white as their Lancashire cheese
to Delph crossroads where the beagles met.

D' you remember the long-legged hares,
tawny as rushes, with flattened ears,
racing in circles round Peacock Hill?
And Spring, green-tongued,
shouting 'Cuckoo!' over Sullom's shoulder
through days alight with gorse and finches' wings?

Here Bleasdale, damson-blue, bristled with heather,
sweeps north
from the slow slope of Fairsnape taking the sun,
ageless as wind and stone.

This country calls us back by roots
deeper than oak and birch,
darker than blood
to a land of belonging.
And always the river
that washed our youth away
runs on and runs forever.

1980   *Phoebe Hesketh*

Old John of Gaunt, time-honour'd Lancaster

Shakespeare, King Richard II, Act 1

THE BILLMEN OF BOWLAND

Against tenfold his numbers on Agincourt's plain,
The gallant King Henry the fight must maintain;
No knight like young Harry had England e'er known,
A pillar of fire to his army he shone;
His troops thronged around him, they darken'd the field,
And the Billmen of Bowland swore never to yield. . . .
. . .the Billmen of Bowland, old Lancashire's pride,
Stood firm on the hills, and the foemen defied. . . .

c1868 *Anon*

FLODDEN FIELD *(the famous history or song)*

All Lancashire for the most part
The lusty Standley stout can lead,
A stock of striplings strong of heart,
brought up from babes with beef and bread.
From Warton unto Warrington,
From Wigan unto Wiresdale,
From Weddecon to Waddington,
From Ribchester unto Rochdale,
From Poulton to Preston with pikes
They with the Standley out forth went.
From Pemberton and Pilling Dikes,
In battle billmen bold were bent.

With fellows fierce and fresh for fight,
Which Halton fields did turn in force;
With lusty lads, liver and light,
From Blackburn and Bolton-in-the-Moors.

16th C. *Anon*

LANCASHIRE

A realm of mountain, forest-haunt, and fell,
And fertile valleys beautifully lone,
Where fresh and far romantic waters roam,
Singing a song of peace by many a cottage home.

c1845   *John Critchley Prince*

LANCASHIRE FARE

Hot Ribble shrimps, lemon-spiked
swimming pinkly
in melted butter.
Or winter broths, thick enough
to cradle spoons,
or morning mushrooms
picked field-fresh.

To follow a winter's walk
a piled-up plate
of bursting flavour,
Lancashire hot-pot,
lavish with lamb
crisp with potatoes
pungent with onions.

With added oysters
for a posher nosh.
Or sliced black-pudding
rich with pig's blood,
or Trawler pie, or kedgeree.
Robust fare to line
a hungry stomach.

Then, for the sweeter tooth
hot Eccles cakes, puffed up with butter
crowded with currants,
hot treacle loaf,
Lancashire Wakes cake
sparkling with sugar.
Food for sharp appetites.

Nouvelle Cuisine unknown.

1995   *Jean Stanbury*

AN AWKWARD JOURNEY

We sneaked in through the back way
one dim dank January afternoon:
we had made the brave decision
no one talked too much about,
the exchange of the white rose for the red.

There's no countryside over there
dyed-in-the-wool Yorkshire folk told us;
only what was given to you
by that daft Boundary Commission,
you're welcome to it if it helps.

Dropping down the Pennine slopes
through the biting clinging mists
we slipped through Laneshawbridge,
an odd undistinguished gateway
to crown such an important journey.

Strange that county barriers should
still furtively operate
as prized landmarks of imagination
like tripe, clogs and shawls
of the not-so-long-ago.

Relativity is a useful word
it is the key to lots of problems
protects us from dangerous abstractions
shows rivalries for what they are:
a load of exaggerated differences.

1995   *Tony MacDermott*

PENNINE TOWNS

Do what we will, the hills are omnipresent.
They stare at us down steepled back streets,
peer round the corners of blackened warehouses,
vault from spire to spire, leap over viaducts.

As summer sun and shadow chase across
their flanks, tawny with bilberry, they twitch
an ear, cock an eye at us, their prisoners,
who from high windows watch even their ease uneasily.

How can we guess what is happening
behind the flimsy curtain of rain,
or not flinch under their icy glare
when January skies are big with snow?

We cannot trust them, the beautiful beasts
that lie in wait for us where pavements end.
They are primordial, memento of our mortality
whose greenness has the promise of the grave.

1982   *John Ward*

from: **POLY-OLBION**

The right Lancastrian line, it from Yorks issue bare,
The Red-rose, our brave Badge, which in their Helmets ware
In many a bloody field, at many a doubtful fight,
Against the House of Yorke, which bare for theirs the White.

1622   *Michael Drayton*

from: **LANCASHIRE**

It's 'ed a deal o' moither, this Cahnty Palatine of ars.
It's bin fowt in, fowt o'er, plundered, an it's sin it's share o' wars.
Bud th' essence o' these 'appenin's is wod med us wod wi ar,
Thi've composted in its 'istry's soil an' browt us aw t' fla'er.

It's browt up mony an 'eroe, ay, an' mony a villain too,
An' it's sired sum o' t' Royalty, an' bred a King er two,
An' t' spirit o' wod 'appened t' them, er wod thi browt t' pass,
Is i' th' 'earts that's beatin' in each lanky lad an' lass.

It's browt up plain an' fancy fooak, like its tradesmen an' its squires,
Bud it's famous fer its experts that warn't fon in other Shires,
Thi wer t' weyvers in its mills, i' t' days of Owd King Cotton,
An' 'appen thers nooan nahadays, bud thi'll never bi fergotton.

Wi've cleyned it up a bit nah, an' weshed its sooty face,
An' thi 'ardly look t' same features frae its cotton factry days,
Bud it warn't o' muck an' chimneys, even in its days o' yore,
Wi've allus 'ed green 'ills an' fells, an' miles o' rollin' moor.

Wi've geet ar streams an' rivers, flashin' an' splashin' dahn t' t' sea,
An' miles an' miles o' sandy shore, wi' its seabirds wild an' free,
An' acre upon acre o' fields of ooats an' corn,
As ripple wen th' wind blows, like gowden seawaves in a storm.

1995   *Michael May*

PENNINES

The spread stone town lies quiet as the light.
From some points you can look right down on it,
The valley sides being steep; an almost
Aerial view at the cost of pulled thighs.

Rooftops mark the lines of streets like the splayed
Spine of a fish. Early separate smokes
Finger the air over the houses, still
Wavering and uncertain in the bright

Morning, before their solidarity
Weaves a sunproof jacket for today's use.
To move out of that valley is to glide
Along the bottom where the railway ran

And over no-man's land to the next one
Just like it. Unless you clamber instead
Sideways, driving your legs beyond the streets
To stumble up among the tussocks here,

Where now in a chilling sweat you can sit
And spit on those rooftops if you want to,
Or lie and listen to the moorbirds when
They shout their mating noises in the wind.

No roads come up this way against the lie
Of the land. You have to come cross-country.
And there on the opposite hill a wall
Arches itself like a startled eyebrow.

1978　　　　　　　　　　　　*John Cassidy*

SNOW FROM THE NORTH

Tonight, snow comes squalling from the north:
It curfews streets to silence,
Smothers footsteps, car tyres, voices
From the golden doorways of pubs.

Driving into flickering ice-flames,
Rooftops are preened with cold's plumage;
Headlights glance on white wings
That beat in steady sweeps of snow.

The road dips and turns, brakes slew the car
Into invisible bends, tyres lurch
As it climbs in an agonising gear
On a hilltop where drifts bury the moor.

Below, lines of yellow lights waft out,
Wind spins its flakes over Burnley;
The town falls asleep, house by house,
Surrendering to the white bird's dreams.

Dead trees lean out from the dark:
Headlights amaze their eyeless staring,
Their lost souls clamour in the wiper blades,
Hiss under the tyres' treachery.

Only my hands between this and me:
They poke out from the grey cuffs of my coat,
Wrenching the car away where it swerves
Towards oblivion.

I'm home, those wings still kissing my face:
Up behind that window she's sleeping, not knowing
I'm here at last - still breathing, still holding
My breath - as snow lets that first star through.

1992   *Graham Mort*

MARTIN MERE, IN LATE NOVEMBER

Farmers' potato fields flooded into wetlands,
designed by the Wildfowl Trust for keen
birdwatchers to tick numbers - Widgeon,
Pintail, Shroveller, Teal, maybe the odd Gadwall.

I watch expectantly, focus the lens -
Greylag geese feed among Whooper
and Berwick swans; trumpeting
their winter arrival.

A voracious enigmatic Snipe
probes its long bill for worms,
a flamed raybeam highlights
the Widgeons' foreheads; like a Spartan

phalanx standing to attention.
Then a bolting Peregrine startles
the serene multitudes;
cloudy wings erupt tumultuous

into the vermilion sunset.
Next to me, cameras aim, then fire;
smiling faces point and sigh
after it's over. Wildfowl of Eden.

1995   *Alan Doherty*

SOUTHPORT BY NIGHT

Respected lady, I took tea with you
This afternoon on your tree-lined avenue,
And you were soignee, charming; promised
Quiet slumber in your arms.

But how my heart's blood batters
At its walls. As your eyes close
I slip from these white sheets across
Your promenade to sands that draw men down.

I kick and run. The gypsy music of the wind
Whisks me along to where
Out on the sea the moon-in-waiting writhes
And I must drown.

1995   *Frances Nagle*

AT FORMBY

From that wide empty shore,
No foot had ever trod before
(Or since the sea drew back the tide),
I climbed the dune's soft slide
To where no higher than my hand
Wind-bitten pines grew in the clogging sand.

But farther from the beach
The trees rose up beyond my reach,
And as I walked, they grew still taller
And I myself smaller and smaller,
Till gazing up at a high wood
I felt that I had found my lost childhood.

1936   *Andrew Young*

ORMSKIRK BORDERS

And on a rise
of roots and moss,
the quarry ends,
well overrun.

A sandstone town
was unearthed here,
its paths disperse
towards elsewhere.

Some underpin
an upland arc,
where fields succeed
or towns might be,

and others merge
where railways died,
on mounds that lie
like boundaries.

Behind all this
goes Lancashire.
The farms run down,
the walls are wide

and where it lay
it ends, and there
where sunsets rise,
the city flares.

1995   *Will Daunt*

EAST LANCASHIRE ROAD, A580

Straight as a Roman road from A to B
through flat-pack fields, brown-wrapped or greyish-green,
a hinterland of the humming city,

this tape of tarmac stretches thirty miles.
Driving my metal cell, thoughts start and stop,
link to feelings, surge, seize up like brakes.

The winter sky is blank, an empty screen;
faceless factories line the road like crates.
I'm moving through, controlled by red or green.

Some fields surprise with sections of sad crops
dulled by the diesel air. I think of vines
dark yet luxuriant on Alpine slopes

where summer's bright as light on glaciers
and - lovers then - we saw the high garden
set in hot rock at freezing altitudes.

Here black ice lacquers the unbending road -
I've gone through lights, but were they green or red?
Perhaps I've crashed: now dead, driving forward

in my afterlife - this unending road.
From factories, fields, sky, no living sign -
only the traffic's physical demand.

1992   *Gladys Mary Coles*

OLD RHYME

Irk, Irwell, Medlock and Tame
When they do meet with Mersey
Do lose their name.

from: **LIVERPOOL: A PROLOGUE**
(for the opening of the Theatre Royal)

Where Mersey's stream long winding o'er the plain,
Pours his full tribute to the circling main,
A band of fishers chose their humble seat;
Contented labour blessed the far retreat:
Inured to hardship, patient, bold, and rude,
They braved the billows for precarious food:
Their straggling huts were ranged along the shore,
Their nets and little huts their only store.

At length fair Commerce found the chosen place,
And smiled approving on the industrious race....

1772   *George Perry*

LIVERPOOL, 1777
(from: Mount Pleasant)

How numerous now her thronging buildings rise!
What varied objects strike the wandering eyes!
Where rise yon masts her crowded navies ride,
And the broad rampire checks the beating tide;
Along the beach her spacious streets extend,
Her areas open, and her spires ascend;
In loud confusion mingled sounds arise,
The docks re-echoing with the seamen's cries,
The massy hammer sounding from afar,
The bell slow-tolling, and the rattling car;
And thundering oft the cannon's horrid roar
In lessening echoes dies along the shore.

There with the genuine glow of Commerce fir'd,
Her anxious votaries plod the streets untir'd....
Now o'er the wondering world her name resounds,
From Northern climes, to India's distant bounds...

(The Africa Trade - Slaves)
Shame to Mankind! But shame to Britons most,
Who all the sweets of Liberty can boast;
Yet deaf to every human claim, deny
That bliss to others which themselves enjoy. . .
The trembling limbs with galling iron bind,
Nor loose the heavier bondage of the mind....

1777   *William Roscoe*

COTTON RHYMES

1. They bought themselves new traps and drags,
   They smoked the best cigars;
   And as they walked the Exchange Flags,
   They thanked their lucky stars.

2. Yes, Great King Cotton's been and gone,
   And cleaned his subjects out,
   And those who trusted him the most,
   Have vanished up the spout.

mid 19th C. *Anon*

from: **A MASQUE OF LIVERPOOL**

I am the English sea-queen; I am she
Who made the English wealthy by the sea.

The street of this my city is the tide
Where the world's ships, that bring my glory, ride.

Far as the tide along my highway swings,
The iron of my shipwrights clangs and rings.

Far inland as the gulls go are my stores,
Where the world's wealth is lockt with iron doors.

And these my merchants gather day by day
The wealth I bring, the wealth I send away.

1930 *John Masefield*

THE COMING IN OF ANCESTORS

Here are the strangers with shabby holdalls
and pale enigmatic smiles:
they disembark, looking around uncertainly
as cloud shadows move
on the moving Mersey;
and what they bring
is partly left at terminals;
and what they say
is scarcely comprehended.

Here are the docks, alive with arrivals,
cargoes of Irish, Germans, Poles.
Are they prepared
for what this land will give?
Will they, the foreigners,
ever feel they belong?
Perhaps not until their blood is passing
in the veins of English grandchildren.

My grandfather merges now
in the whisper of their lives:
his Scandinavian father
that whiskered man at chess
in the old, newly discovered photograph,
naturalised and with suitably altered name -
did he, as he slowly moved the chess pieces,
recall the forests, the fiords, the frozen winters?

My grandmother remembers her own:
Italian, in black toque hat,
wearing bright carnelian beads.

Here is their Liverpool -
the landfall in the west,
waterfront, heartland, home.

1984   *Gladys Mary Coles*

LIVERPOOL 8, 1942

It was run down even then,
but still possessed an elegance
and faded charm;
wide streets with politicians' names
and broken fanlights
over doors of peeling paint -
town houses of the merchant class
let off in rooms to passing trade.

What rooms they were,
they must have seen
fine ladies in their hoops and silks
and gentlemen in gold brocade
turning the pages as the ladies played,
while at the docks lay ships
which brought the wealth -
triangle trade of cotton, guns and slaves.

Time running out in days of war
with shore leave passing soon,
love was too self-absorbed to see
the cornered ghosts in that high-ceilinged room.
Now, half a century more,
among the shadows in these cornices
lurk other shades,
of Youth and Love and War.

1995 *Betty Jones*

DIRECTIONS *(Bootle)*

With a war to forget, we grew up
on what was left of something, weeds
on battered ground where houses once had stood:

plantain tough as boots, irascible dock,
dogged dandelion, and come-up-smiling rose-
bay willow-herb among strewn bricks;

streets of tar and cobble
with dusty corner shops
and lamp-posts you could swing on -

ropes that smelt of creosote and ships:
a centripetal spin into a vicious hug of iron,
a centrifugal jerk to outer space.

1990 *Matt Simpson*

HIGH WINDOWS *(Bootle)*

No mines but always coal;
the smell of coal
and the smack in the mouth
of gas across black hills.
And, further on, squat dockside
cranes, their lines spun out
into the grey Mersey.

Bootle this,
backstreet upon backstreet
upon backstreet and gaps
like missing teeth.
A hard-case place, proud
of its bomb-scars,
of its fires in blitztime.

And here, from the highest
windows, above the sudden squares of grass,
the speckle of fog-lights poking
through the shapes of streets, I am
drawn to absences,
to spaces in the air
where buildings pressed and steam
blew from slithering trains once,
where songs from pubs and parlours
rose and burst, and slow men
tugged horses, ringing hooves,
over grinding lanes.

1993   *Brian Wake*

LIVERPOOL *after William McGonagall*

O Liverpool on the Mersey River
Noble city, how I shiver
With pride at the thought of your history
And your great men who are gone
Like Huskisson, and Mr Gladstone.
After each you have named a dock
From Bootle to the Liver clock
And some miles further on,
Even to Dingle and gay Garston.

You are the second greatest port in all the land,
And your population runs to eight hundred thousand.

Twenty miles of busy docking
Thanks to all the good men working
On them. The brave stevedores
And men in crane-driving
Have helped to make this great port thriving.

Your flour mills and other famous industries,
Biscuit, pea, soap, and sugar factories,
All play a very important part;
And of all industrial south-west Lancashire,
Liverpool is the very heart.
Noble city astride the River Mersey,
I am sure we all salute thee.

1967   Roger McGough

from the song:

In my Liverpool home, in my Liverpool home
We speak with an accent exceedingly rare
Meet under a statue exceeedingly bare
And if you want a cathedral we've got one to spare
In my Liverpool home.

c.1970   Peter McGovern

CODA TO THE CIVIL WAR

Where the Mersey coils a serpentine stain
Through a twilit shire, through a skirmished land
Where a dislodged crown is the fireweed's gain
And a dying oath gags the lost command
Then the horsemen turn to the roads of pain
Warrington's key bridge sees the evening spanned
Hollow hooves clash back across mire and rain
And the county cries under Cromwell's hand.

From the priest-town rout to the Alt's floodplain
Watch the remnants flee from their final stand
To the fringe they ride, the map lined with slain
And a dying oath gags the lost command
Now the trudging troops of the King's campaign
Become riven ranks and retreats unplanned
Yet their agony strung up on dusk remains
Still the county cries under Cromwell's hand.

By Maghull's black wall, and on Newton's lane
Mounts will melt at dawn, cavaliers of sand
Feathers, manes, in mist, tight the desperate rein
And a dying oath gags the lost command
Where the future's torn from a Royalist brain
There the horse is cursed and the rider damned
See the musket, sword, and the ghosts unlain
Where the county cries under Cromwell's hand.

1995   *John Calvert*

CAT-I'-TH'-WINDOW *(a cottage near Standish)*

If he was seeking shelter   King Charles had his spaniel
He knew that the coast was clear   To guard him from all fear
  By the sign in a lighted window   When Cromwell's men were stalking
A cat for a Cavalier.   Cats watched for a Cavalier.

1995   *Margaret Ross*

Between Standish and Parbold is a cottage with three black cats carved on the gable end - a reminder that here was a refuge for the Royalists in the Civil War, when a statue of a black cat was placed in the window if the area was safe from Roundhead troops.

THE RAINHILL TRIALS *(October 1829)*

The iron-clad monsters
Stood to attention
Spurting so much smoke
That even the most ferocious
Of dragons would have turned and run.

Crowds gathered at a safe distance.
They'd heard such tales of these creatures -
That cows dropped dead
In their speedy wake;
But worse much worse.

That they swallowed people whole
Through gaps in their sides
And swept them away
To far-off lands
Never to return.

Now here the baying beasts
Waited. Tamed and shackled
Straining to prove that they
Were the best and would
Have that place in history.

The *Cyclopede* ran well
At first, but faded fast.
While the *Novelty* sped
Quickly on, amazing watchers
Until its bellows burst.

The mighty *Sanspareil*
Charged on, until 'wounded'
It retired, weeping water
From a failed pump, then
Perseverance ran out of steam.

The ungainly *Rocket* stood proud
In victory, the judges satisfied,
Opposition defied. It moved forward
Knowing that we would
All follow on these 'right lines'.

1995   **Sue Gerrard**

RED BLOOD RIVER *(Sankey Brook)*

Memory's soft focus dulls my mind.
It must have been in 1932,
give or take a childhood year,
when we explored the Red Blood River,
Sonny Baxter and I.

The Ordnance Survey map reads Sankey Brook,
prompts thoughts of sparkling stream
through scented meadowlands,
of netted sticklebacks in jam-jars,
daisy chains.

Reality then was stinking effluent,
from factory making coloured cellophane,
colours varied with the week's production run.
Our favourite was the scarlet, for we knew
that back upstream,
between the heaps of chemiwaste,
back there in Dead Man's Gulch,
there lay the bodies of the U.S. Cavalry,
slain in their dozens by the arrows of the Sioux.

We knew, Sonny Baxter and I,
for had we not seen it
at the Scala Cinema last week?
Black and white it may have been.
We thought in colour.

The brook flowed on
beyond the radius of ten-year legs
into the flat-capped, flat-accented,
flat fields of Lancashire,
side by side with its eponymous and derelict canal
corrupted on its way by hostile factories
seeking refuge in big sister Mersey.

Our sanctuary lay beyond those murky mountains,
through hostile Injin lands
to boiled eggs and jammy toast.
I'm told the paper-works closed down,
something about 'environment', they said.
The canal's been 'heritaged' by sturdy volunteers.
I must go back to see the Red Blood River.
I suppose it's been rejuvenated.
Unlike Sonny Baxter and I.

1995   *Albert Morgan*

WINWICK CHURCH

The church at little Winwick,
It stands upon a sod,
And when a maid is married there,
The steeple gives a nod.

Alas! how many ages,
Their rapid flight have flown,
Since on that high and lofty spire
There's moved a single stone.

Trad

WARRINGTON ALE

Your doctors may boast of their lotions,
And ladies may talk of their tea;
But I envy them none of their potions:
A glass of good stingo for me.
The doctor may sneer if he pleases,
But my recipe never will fail;
For the physic that cures all diseases
Is a bumper of Warrington ale.

1875   *Anon*

from: BEWSEY *(Bewsey Hall)*

But yet th' historic page records a tale,
Crimson'd with blood, when ev'n these stately walls,
As yet uninjur'd by the shocks of time,
Could not the sword of massacre repel
From their own guarded Lord; for civil strife
Bade here dark Murder his fell poignard steep
In the defenceless breast. A hireling band
At dead of night, when nature sunk to rest,
And sleep secure had those proud tow'rs disarm'd
Hither insideous stole....
For ah! unarm'd, and in his bed surpris'd,
Vilely they butcher'd the devoted Lord!
Meanwhile a servant-maid, with pious guile,
Bore in her apron, artfully conceal'd,
The infant heir; and many a danger brav'd,
Saved him uninjur'd from the ruffians' swords,
The Negro's valour fav'ring her escape.

19th C.   *John Fitchett*

THE COLLIERY EXPLOSION, HAYDOCK
June 7th, 1878

200 lives were lost. This anonymous ballad was composed and sold as a penny broadsheet to raise money for the widows and orphans

Weep mothers, weep o'er the loss of your dear ones
The Fathers and Children who are strewn amongst the dead,
The Explosion has fill'd the whole district with sadness
For homes that are lonely, and hearts that have bled.

My partner is gone, and my children are missing -
Sobs a heartbroken Mother in agony wild;
Great God, can it be? We are parted for ever,
Shall I never more see my dear husband and child.

'Twas but early today, they left our own dwelling,
Me thought they seem'd happy, contented and free:
How he'd spend his Whit week my poor boy was telling,
As he bound away with his innocent glee.

He oft join'd in play with youthful companions,
In the hedges and lanes, he delighted to roam
It seems strange to me, that my poor lad has perish'd
Whilst his bosom companions are happy at home.

My dear husband kissed the sweet lips of our baby
In sorrow I think of it now 'tis past,
He bade us as usual a hearty good morning,
Nor thought for a moment it would be his last....

There are sorrowing ones in the neighbourhood of Haydock,
God grant to them, His help may be given;
Though the present be dark may Hope fill the bosom,
That at last they shall meet with their lov'd ones in Heaven.

1878   *Anon*

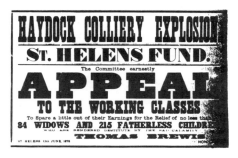

THE WINDLE WITCH - ISOBEL ROBY

When darkness falls and day is wrapped away,
Some say I take strange shapes and appear
In a thousand guises, to stalk around the
Town and put fear into every heart.
A dog, a cat, a foal, a fawn. People
See in me the evil which is
Simply a reflection of what
Lies within their own
Embittered hearts. I am
In short the image of
The devil, which
They themselves do
Make for
Others

BUT
It
Is I
Who will pay
The penalty for false
Word and thought and deed.
It is said I have the Devil's power
Even so I am captive here amongst the
Living dead. My only consolation is
In the non-confessing voice which sounds
Strangely like my own. If I had the
Devil's power I would cast a spell on all
Of you and be free to live another day and
Watch the sand flow through for yet another hour.

1995   *Sue Gerrard*

Isobel Roby of Windle, St Helens, was tried at Lancaster Castle on Wednesday, August 19th, 1612 - the same day as the famed Lancashire Witches, (the Demdikes and the Chattoxes) and although not connected in any way, was found guilty of Witchcraft and was hanged with them.

BOGGARTS ABOUND

The dictionary says:
apparition, hobgoblin or ghost;
and when it comes to mischief,
boggarts cause the most -

Hackenshall, Hothershall,
Clegg Hall, Sykes Lumb Farm,
all their nasty little tricks
cause a lot of harm. . .

Noisy little creatures,
drumming on oak chests,
smashing up cream pitchers,
making people vexed,

Shaking the bed hangings,
or dragging covers off;
but then they'll do some farm work,
stacking up the crops. . .

Make a grab for your leg
as you climb the stairs,
snatch the baby, leave him
on the hearth for a scare.

Some can even change shape:
rabbit, dog or cat,
or it may be something
scarier than that.

And the tale is often told
how at Boggart Hole Clough,
one family had to leave,
they'd just about had enough.

As they reached the corner,
cart laden with fixtures and fittings. . .
up popped the boggart, grinning:
'Ay, neighbours, we're flitting!'

1995　　　　　　*Carole Baldock*

'Boggart' may derive from 'burgh ghaist' (town ghost);
it is said to have 'great lung arms, and a whiskin' tail, and hair as
black as soot, and rolling een as big as saucers'.

PENNINGTON FLASH

A mile or so from the East Lancs Road
Bordered by pit heads and shafts
Wedged in grooves between mounds of black ash
Lies Pennington Flash

A hard-earned gritty legacy
Bequeathed by miners' sweat
A rich inheritance of water and space
Above the coal face

The yacht club's coloured tilting sails
Balloon above the ash
Dip and weave across the lake
Ripples in their wake

Moorhens and coots share reedy homes
With warblers and frogs
A hungry mallard and her brood
Search for food

Boys in boots and anoraks
Settle in bird hides and watch
As crested grebes and herons splash
In Pennington Flash

1995   *Sheila Clift*

OVER BILLINGE LUMP

The anaemic February sun,
low in an ice-blue sky,
struggles in vain to blunt the north wind,
cutting across snow-crusted fields,
nipping our ears.

Tiptoeing though farmyard slutch,
we pass abandoned chicken-sheds,
ghosts of decaying P.O.W. huts.
The doberman snarls and leaps,
straining at its chain.
Will the staple in the wall hold firm?

We climb the hill.
Bright green shoots of winter wheat
pierce the melting snow.
Boots slip and slide,
seeking purchase in the claggy earth.

At the top the old stone hut,
disfigured now by vandals' 'art',
triggers memories of childhood picnics.

The latticed towers stand silent,
Christmas trees of silvery steel
festooned with snow-white saucers
and sonic candelabra,
silent, that is, to our untutored ear.

What ultra short-wave messages
are winging through the innocent air,
as 'Someone Out There' goes about our business
without so much as a 'by our leave'.

1995   *Albert Morgan*

OUR ONLY FATHER AND SON OUTING
(Haigh Hall)

Our bus stop: Aspull.
So we shuffle and stagger,
monkeys swinging through a fog
of Woodbines, Capstan Full Strengths.

My excitement was a pack of horses
pulling him along the cobbled lane
past a set of white houses;
in the mouth of the countryside.

The first time for both of us:
at the ghost-house of Haigh Hall
its six pillars opening wide
the entrance where sycamores walk on their palms
and ash leaves insect into corners.

I charged to the miniature train ride,
boasting cartwheels, forward rolls,
stood on my hands against a chestnut tree.

Tiny carriages whizzed me around a giant bracelet
through rhododendrons and green-draped monsters.

That pear-shaped man
in blue trilby, milk-bottom glasses
rumbled along the tarmac.

Together we skimmed flying saucers
under the bridge:
that narrow stretch of Wigan canal
other kids could dive in.

It was the only time dad laughed !
Me chasing his coloured pebbles;
the water's circles winking back at me.

1993   *Peter Street*

THE WAY WE WERE IN 1900: WIGAN PIER

Roll up, roll up, all the fun of the fair!
See the fat lady, cross the gypsy's palm!
Don't be shy now, smile, it's Wakes Week!
Stroll the tarted pier, just smell that air!

Round a corner there's a grimy street,
A mine where dirt-streaked dummies toil.
At each half-hour in a two-up-two-down
An actor squares up to his 'old man's ' death.
'He 'ad the black spit, and so he 'anged hissel'.

A child clunks a dolly peg, someone mutters
'They think it's a thing to play with'.
Off to tea and cakes in the 'George Orwell Rooms',
Over her shoulder she adds
'It was bloody 'ard work, luv'.

One floor down a queue becomes Class Four
Drilled into school under arches marked
'Girls', 'Boys'. They wriggle on benches,
Stammer out Mental Arithmetic, Read Aloud.
Hands are rapped for jewellery, or dirty nails.

Now it's Handkerchief Inspection! At the held
Pointing cane grandmas tremble, faces drop.
Eyeing Miss, one sneaks a Kleenex to each friend.

Everywhere, groups of them bend
Permed heads, pick over half-familiar things
That gobbled up their youth.

1995   *Angela Topping*

LANCASHIRE TEXTILE POEM

Cambrics, wigans, twills,
Piques, madapoloma,
Dhoutis, ducks and drills,
Listadoes, bafts, macanas.
Bramantes, ginghams, sheeting,
Domestics, salempores,
Reginas, zephyrs, ticking,
Nainsooks, Morocco shawls.
Haircloth, fodens, flannelette,
Batistes, checks, gaberdine,
Denim, mulls, jeanettes,
Pongees and sateen.

1995   *Daphne Schiller*

PIT BROW LASSIES, ATHERTON 1918

The third girl in this group, she smiles, cocksure
Her mates are wary of the camera's stare.
All cowled like nuns - the dirt streaking the pure,
A bond of sisterhood in linked arms there.
Learned helplessness which sifts out the demure
As dust descends from screen to slackened air.
A century turns, they look out - wonder-struck,
Their sixfold clogs scraped free of Chowbents' muck.

1995   *John Calvert*

A LANCASHIRE HAIKU

Rain-worn cobblestones
Underline derelict mills
And no clogs clatter.

1995   *Lance Cleary*

THE LAMPLIGHTERS

At evening they made their rounds.
The streets knew them.
Those sturdy solid men
With poles across their shoulders
Carrying a whisper of light.

The unhurried walk.
The last lit lamp behind.
Striding into darkness.
Then a pause.
A falling circle of light
Dismissing their long shadows
To a pool of dusk on the pavement.

They have gone.
And we, who stand in the space
Between the light of birth
And the unlit lamp of death,
Must light our own lamps.

1995　　　　　　　*W.A. Mellors*

ON A VISIT TO SALFORD'S MINING MUSEUM

I can remember pits and men who said
how much they detested to grovel
on their bellies, to pick-axe coal for
not enough money to live from week
to week. Who made their sons get themselves
a trade. Who died from silicosis.

I also remember outrage when
the mines shut down leaving half of the town
unemployed. And I could never make
out why they put up such a fight to
save something that had destroyed countless
generations of fellow workers.

1995　　　　　　　*Eileen Holroyd*

WALKING DAY (*Whit Walk*)

At the back of the Chapel
on the shadow side,
girls in white dresses
flutter about on the dirt road
like butterflies in a cabbage patch.
Waxen narcissus and stiff blue iris
swing in their wicker baskets
as they eye each other excitedly.
Who has the prettiest dress?
The whitest shoes?

Over the fence on the cricket pitch,
a lark rises into the Saturday sky
matching their excitement
with its trembling wings.
Suddenly, from the Chapel gates
the band strikes up
a loud brass signal
for the girls to go into the sunshine.

Today the road is theirs.
They are princesses in a royal procession,
shy and proud in their white dresses,
their young hearts banging to the drums.

People lean on garden gates to watch them pass
and the old women sit in the doorways,
nodding and smiling.
A sober line of Chapel folk walk behind
under the blue banner that rocks above their heads,
where the good shepherd points them
with his finger to the Monument.

Down all the house-lined streets
to this one place
processions come.
The joyfully discordant noise
of different brass bands fills the air.
They stand together to proclaim their faith.
'Sabbath Schools are England's Glory'
swells in a mighty chorus round the square.

1995   *Deirdre Armes Smith*

STRETFORD

Looking through the café window grille
beyond the fence of heavy iron spikes
the view is of the electric grid

I stir an over-sweetened mug of tea
while scanning the uncrossable road
from Old Trafford to the Motorway

Green and grim is the ancient tree,
seeded back in cartwheel days,
that blocks now the cumulus cloudscape

1987   *Gerald England*

OLD TRAFFORD *(Lancashire Cricket Club)*

And a ghostly batsman plays to the bowling of a ghost,
And I look through my tears at a soundless clapping host
As the run-stealers flicker to and fro,
O my Hornby and my Barlow long ago....

1893   *Francis Thompson*

MANCHESTER TO BOLTON

Between blackened walls beside the railway track
and corrugated iron of Viking's Boiler-Making Yard
two almond trees blossom white tears.

By road there's frontages on view, by rail the back
side of everything's exposed; wrecked cars on land cleared
for rebuilding, left vacant fifteen years,

oil drums, scrap metal, coal-hoppers, slim-waisted
cooling towers. Behind a bridge a disturbed
boy, his face streaked with tears, sleeps

away the day he should have been in school. A raised
pickaxe, delicate as a seagull or a child's drawn bird.
Beyond the Irwell's shining waters a willow also weeps.

1980   *John Ashbrook*

A NEW SONG ON THE PETERLOO MEETING

Rise, Britons, rise now from your slumber,
Rise, and hail the glorious day.
Come and be ranked with the number,
With true friends of Liberty.
Don't you see those heroes bleeding,
Lying in their crimson gore?
Britain's sons who died for freedom,
And who fell, to rise no more.

It was the sixteenth day of August,
Thousands met on Peterloo plain,
Where we arrived, of fear regardless,
Little we knew of their dreadful schemes;
When, lo, we spied them near advancing,
With swords drawn, on mischief bent,
Rushed through the crowd with horses prancing,
'Twould make a heart of stone relent.

But matchless Hunt, that valiant hero,
His name it shall recorded be;
Says he: 'My friends, I'll never leave you,
Though death be my destiny'.
Straight to New Bailey then they brought him,
In a dungeon close confined;
Then to Lanacaster they did send him,
For conspiracy, as I've been told.

Britannia's sons, so famed for bravery,
Who fought so bold for Freedom's cause,
Now you're doomed to cruel slavery,
And oppressed by so many laws.
So, Britons, let's no longer greet them,
But endeavour to be free.
Let the air resound and echo:
Shouts of Hunt, likewise Wolseley.

c1819   *Anon*

Peterloo plain: an area of open land near the centre of Manchester, called St. Peter's Field; now part of St. Peter's Square.
Henry Hunt, radical MP, was to have addressed the meeting, but was arrested and imprisoned.
Sir Charles Wolseley was a supporter of the radicals.

*On Two Millers of Manchester, named Bone and Skin,
who wanted to Monopolize Corn*

Two millers thin,
Called Bone and Skin,
Would starve us all, or near it;
But be it known
To Skin and Bone,
That Flesh and Blood can't bear it.

18th C.　　　　　　　　　　*John Byrom*

THE SCENES OF MANCHESTER

The scenes of Manchester I sing,
Where the arts and sciences are flourishing;
Where smoke from factory chimneys bring
The air so black, so thick and nourishing.
Where factories that by steam are gated,
And children work half suffocated,
It makes me mad to hear folk, really,
Cry: 'Manchester's improving daily'.

19th C.　　　　　　　　　　*Anon*

THE MANCHESTER SHIP CANAL

Oh, the *SS Irwell* left this port the stormy sea to cross,
They heaved the lead and went ahead on a voyage to Barton Moss.
No fairer ship e'er left the slip from this port to Natal,
Than the boats that plough the waters of the Manchester Canal.

1888　　　　　　　　　　　　　　*RSK*

VALETTE IN MANCHESTER

Mr Monsieur wore dark hats, sombre suits,
was sad, quiet, kindly and shy;
earned his living at the School of Art
teaching Life Class to draw with finger and thumb;
twenty years, craved Provence, clear light,
red poppies in cornfields, shimmering seas;
grieved to watch his Brazilian wife waste
and die in foreign parts under cold hills.

Stuck it out to catch on canvas, drop
by drop, the last honey from our streets:
trams, hansom cabs, long skirts, barrowboys,
golden cobblestones in Albert Square,
Mersey flats moored under Bailey Bridge,
smoke dissolving railway arches at blue dusk,
the mystery of fog on still canals.

Passed on a pupil greater than himself,
a cold-eyed giant whose city has no shadows
where fogs are shrouds and every man is an island.

1990   *John Ward*

Adolphe Valette is honoured in Manchester both
for his own painting and as teacher of L.S. Lowry.

BEN BRIERLEY (1825-96)

When I wrote my first dialect poem
The critics said: 'Take more spelling lessons;
We think you've got Dyslexia'. Back home
I cried all night, and searched for the reasons
Behind Brierley's success. Manchester's
Famous 'Dyslexic' poet, with an inn
Named after him, which sells beer to punters
Who know little of their poet's rhymin'.
From his pub-sign Ben's pen swings in the wind
As he dreams up one last verse; but there's
No more (dr)ink for him...I am determined
That one drunkard will think of him, so here's
To you, Ben. Di'lect's lost on me, but cheers.

1995   *Arthur Chappell from:* **HOME TOWN** (*Ashton under Lyne*)

Riding over Chat Moss in the train
A waft of celery through the open window
Carries me home to Ashton-under-Lyne.
I feel again beneath my feet
The cobbles of the market square
Jostle with baskets, elbows, broad-aproned bosoms,
Weave among banners of dress lengths and
Curtain cloth, stacks of tomatoes, onions,
Wellingtons, pans, Bill
Sowerbutts' masses of tulips and daffs.
Linger to choose from crisp lettuce bobbing
In vats of cool water, inhale
That evocative celery smell from
Blanched and dripping heads;
Hear the brash barker extolling his china,
His banter competing with jangle of bells
From the kids' roundabout;
Indulge in a ninety-nine, gaze as I lick,
Across to the grey Palladian Town Hall
Where once we waited, interminably waited
In incessant rain; all the town's school-children
Packed into squares, clutching a Union Jack
Each in a sticky hand, waiting
To see the King arrive....

Summer afternoons when classroom stifled
We would stand on the railway bridge,
Watch engines shunting in the National sidings,
Thrill to the serial rattle and clatter
Of wagons connecting, taste the acrid smoke.
A quick scamper over to the green Moss;
Among the market gardens,
Pale skinny children for a rare half hour
Would roll in grass and daisies.

Home: mucky old Ashton,
Like a raddled old woman, wearing
The surprising fresh fragrance
Of celery.

1995   *Mary Brett*

THE IRK

This simple river has been here
soaking its aquatic soul
long before man first set foot
on higher ground surmounting
all the marsh around.

Not much to shout about
on its few miles of lonely life
from foothills of the Pennines
to the Irwell's silent mouth;
except the small secluded park
laid out with formal lawns,
paved walks and flower beds;
where the medieval hall stood
mellowing its honeyed walls.

Now a natural landscape
is re-created on its banks,
with a thin screen of birches,
the wildnesses of grass;
here too the peaceful water
only once in modern times
reached high above itself
and snatched a man.

Death's hint of drama too
is lost when the river quits
this wild idyllic spot
to join the toilers in the town,
where they discard its rural past
with quaint industrial artefacts:
old tyres, split mattresses and prams
they fished the baby out of long ago.

1990   *John David Mallinson*

OLDHAM: DECEMBER

The wind that whistles over Oldham Edge,
having crossed the town,
the road, the railway and
the demolished wastes of Glodwick,
hits me full in the face on Hardy Street.
I turn down Barlow, South Hill, Chief Streets,
find the shelter of Bobbin Skewer Walk.
Mr Khan curses the weather in Urdu;
he has cleared a path
through to the local Mosque
but snow still drifts
threatening to engulf the Pentecostal Church,
Ukrainian Social Club and Old Folks' Flats.
The lake in the park is frozen over.
A lone van struggles to climb Park Road,
wheels spinning in the salt-green slush.
The winter isolates inhabitants;
few venture out for fish and chips,
prawn foo yung or chapattis and curry.
The doors of the Waterloo Inn
are open - just: four players
huddled round the pool table
discuss plans for summer holidays.

1983   *Gerald England*

NEWTON SILK MILL (1832)

Stands back sandblasted
from the dusty Oldham road;
a scrubbed and solid structure,
it has well outlasted
the lesser textile trade.

Architectural detail
of fine stone lintels
over doors and windows
were denied the cotton mills'
economies of scale.

It has long survived
its younger neighbourhood;
rows of selfless dwellings
toiling back to back against
the poverty and grime.

1990   *John David Mallinson*

GOING TO SHAW ON THE TRAIN

Mona and Nile, Raven and Lilac, Briar and Dawn:
working or not, the cotton mills are named
like ships: tall letters calling over distances.

Metal echoes from the old machines
follow us down the rails.
Blue air with a white cloud print
unwinds brick chimneys as we pass.

In Shaw, someone points out the house for me.
The sisters who were murdered there
would have remembered them:

Mona and Nile
Raven and Lilac
Briar and Dawn

in the days of their glory.

1994 *Adèle Geras*

MILLSTONE GRIT

From sullen mounds of battered earth
it thrusts its fists at the universe;
millions of years of compressed dust.

A girl there waits, her lover climbs,
his warm breath on the crusted skin.

The spark the rock emits she's seen
in his eyes in the evening light,
and wonders if the rock might too,
within its own great density, have love,

passed on from clay to flesh
as the fragrance of a rose is,
or the wild flower's essence in a wood,
that would speak of love if an essence could.

1995 *Wendy Bardsley*

ON FINDING JOHN COLLIER'S GRAVE AT ROCHDALE

I climbed 122 steps
To St Chads upon the hill,
Where a winter's chill crept into my bones
And a warmth into my heart -
When I said 'How do' to thee John.
'Jack of all trades master of none' -
Your words not mine,
Weaver, school master, poet,
Painter, engraver, musician;
Father of Lancashire dialect.
Stone and steel guard your ashes well,
But in me a small spark of you lives in.

1990   *Kathleen Johnston*

Kathleen Johnston, nèe Collier, a descendant of John Collier, who wrote as 'Tim Bobbin'.

POSTCARD HOME TO ROCHDALE
from The Lake District

I hope y' like this postcard, love,
Though t' pictures none too grand.
There's lots of water 'ere all right
But they 'aven't got much sand.
And t' weather - well, it's wet as lakes,
First a downpour, then a shower,
An' there's no arcades t' shelter in,
Nor 'musement park, nor Tower.
In fact I'd rather be back 'ome
Wi' canals an' dirty mills,
'Cos there's nowt up 'ere but scenery,
An' y' can't see that fer th' 'ills!

1989   *Ken Craven*

The Goose, the Calf, the little Bee,
Are great on Earth I prove to thee,
And rule the great affairs of Man,
Explain this riddle if thou can.

Old Lancashire Riddle

LANCASHIRE HOBBY-HORSE

Easter-tide, the year rising,
maidens blush at bold youths...
scream, scampering,
pursued by Old Ball.

It's a nightmare:
hidden by a sackcloth sheet,
half-man, half-beast,
galloping back and forth.
He holds up on his stick
the creature's head,
moving its jaw
up and down, up and down.

Old Ball has
eyes of smashed glass,
the bottoms of
broken wine bottles,
a look entirely inhuman.
Snaps with
vicious teeth
made of huge nails.

Rituals die out,
so they say,
nothing lurking
from the bad old days.

1995   *Carole Baldock*

(ritual in Burnley and Blackburn, died out there by the 1840s; persisted in the Swinton and Worsley areas of Manchester)

BOLTON-LE-MOORS, 1960

From Vernon Street in Bolton
you can lift your eyes up to the moors
forgetting traffic, grimed infirmary
and the Blind School where they weave baskets
in compensation.
Between mills' open fingers
you can see them
tawny as sleeping mastiffs
stretch out in the sun.
And Breightmet, rashed with bungalows,
is magical in mist
that kindly scarves a see-through school
with evening amethyst.
Never before in industry's complex
have I felt heather
and wind in the grasses -
the wild and the worked-on working together
spinning the music of mills
from earth's resources.

1989　　　　　　　　　*Phoebe Hesketh*

MOORLAND MILL, NEAR BOLTON

Respite of seventy years had gentled its shape
And stilled the air.
Walls were lichen-stained and ruminant,
Freed from the hammering of looms
And clog-irons' clamour over granite stones.

We sheltered there from slanting Pennine rain.
The children heedless in their playing house -
Upholstered green and bramble-trapped -
Bore in their trophies,
Pebbles from the brook,
(Careful! The reeds are treacherous)
A leather glove, suppliant still,
Its fingers curled.

They start next week, the developers.
Quality houses, lake en suite.

1995　　　　　　*Margaret Woodcock*

RIVINGTON PIKE, GOOD FRIDAY

Lord Leverhulme, who liked surprises,
Created a garden on Rivington Hill -
A hint of ancient Babylon
In the rain-laden air
Of Lancashire.

Terraced pathways wander and wind
Through rhododendrons and rowan trees,
Past fairy-tale follies
And waterfalls.

Breathless flights of sandstone steps
Slippery with the sodden leaves
Of last year, and the year before,
Lead to ornate balconies
With crumbling walls.

Above the trees, the hill's broad shoulders
Spring to the open summit, where
A sturdy monument stands four-square
Offering shelter against the squalls
Of Lancashire wind.

Anoraked families munch their chocolate
Before setting out across the moor
To the T.V. mast on Winter Hill,
Graceful against the watery sky.

Westward, the misty coastline gleams
In a sudden shaft of April sun;
Below, the reservoirs glitter like steel
And Mill Towns litter
The Lancashire Plain.

1994   *Bessie Hall*

RIVINGTON CHURCH
(verse by the incumbent)

Who has not heard of Steeple-Jack
That lion-hearted Saxon?
Though I'm not he, he was my sire
For I am Steeple Jackson

c1870   *Rev. Jackson*

NOVEMBER DAY ON WINTER HILL

Fog-wrapped, we walked, inhabited a dream,
our boots roughstitched a patchwork counterpane
of peat and bog, needled the rough terrain,
worked seeds of cottongrass into the seams.
No wind breathed life, no scissor-sharp sunbeam
dissected damp, dispelled the mizzling rain,
no creatures snuffled undergrowth's domain.
Two fools, we trespassed on an angel's scheme.

There seemed no sky above, nor earth beneath
to lend some substance to the place we trod.
Our fantasies roamed free, bestowed the heath
with supernatural life; a spaceman's pod
slowly descending from the distant stars
to capture humans; carry us to Mars.

Eddying fog revealed transmitter's mast
with cable-slung repair car gliding past.
Our laughter mocked illusion, shrilled relief,
crowing, denied a lingering belief.

1995   *Barbara Horrocks*

ETCHINGS OF LAMBSTOP

Did those stalwart figures come to plunder
The down under their native heath?
With strides so purposeful and clad
        In spattered plaid -
They reached the hill of Holcombe
        And looked down;
'This valley of wild garlic' so they said
        'Will be our town'.
The rural scene that lay before their eyes
Assumed a 'peopling' of spires and
Dwellings, built to honour God and fellow men
Or that was seen within their eyes.
They settled here and soon benificence
And such activity were seen - to span
The valley town and spread across the land
both North and West - a kind of filigree.
With eyes a-twinkle - and hands of steel
These Scots from far-flung Spey
Now had the Irwell drive their wheel;
'Though not' they said,' as large as Spey'
It still served textiles -
The medium of their work and day.
The ram - or tup - could rest his fleece
Beneath the hill that towered and teased
The sun, so giving birth to light and shade.
The ewe gave birth up on the hill - and there
The lambs lay strewn and white
In blessed innocence of future plight.
These men, these Grants, a 'Square' they made
And there caused printing, fine and true
To be transferred to calico - from here
To Manchester and all North West dens
of Haute Couture.
Success was as a flag they flew
Not just their own - but other's too.
Their character imprints the town they made
Their own - and still today - the echoes
Like a deja vu haunt hill and brook
Street and passage too.
Brothers Grant, rams and lambs, mills and men
        Salute you!

1995   *Deirdre Woodcock*

THE IRWELL FORGE BAND
PLAYING ON HOLCOMBE HILL

Brass instruments coiled
into tubes of sunlight,
uniforms green as distance,
rumpled fields and hills.

Peel Tower standing there;
a clarinet on its bell,
the wind tuning low notes,
from high windows.

People coming together
uplifted by the wind,
the sounds of sunlight,
this afternoon fellowship.

Breezy talk mingling
with notes and laughter,
bright sounds everywhere
in concert together.

Cotton grass swaying
to the rhythm of the wind,
conducting the light
with delicate brilliance.

The wind arranging clouds,
shuffling sheet music,
linking handfuls of sound,
dancing round the hill.

1993　　　　*Chris Woods*

from
HOLCOMBE POEM/POEM FOR A GIRL I DIDN'T MEET

walking on the moors thinking about how I didn't meet
　　　you yesterday
heather underfoot and mist over Pendle
the moor changing like an animal/brown to green grey to
　　　purple with the weather
sky blue at the edges
　　　　　like a letter that came too late. . . .

1967　　　　　　　　　　　　　　*Adrian Henri*

ROSSENDALE

Rossendale Forest, Lancashire: an oath once taken by every inhabitant, at the age of 12

You shall true Liege-man be,
Unto the King's Majestie:
Unto the beasts of the Forest you shall no hurt do,
Nor to anything that doth belong thereunto;
The offences of others you shall not conceal,
But, to the utmost of your power, you shall them reveal
Unto the Officers of the Forest,
Or to them who may see them redrest:
All these things you shall see done,
So help you GOD at his Holy Doom.

Anon

ROSSENDALE

The view of distant hills
Was kept for Sundays,
When the valley chimneys,
All six score of them,
If you could see to count,
Would only trickle smoke
From damped-down furnaces.
Time for worship, walks and prospect
Of the only proper dinner of the week.

By eight o'clock on Mondays,
Clouds were back, precipitating soot,
Reducing splendid Sabbath colours
To their customary grey.
I remember, even now, the thrill
Of finding that the inside of a brick
Was red.

1995   *Brian Mitchell*

VALLEY OF THE KINGS
The Pet Crematorium, Rossendale

You tread a narrow lane,
Before you stumble upon it:
a patch of lamb's breath.
Ground mint fresh
and the sleeping vale
lying high above the quarry
and grey brick.

Can you hear a rose tree whimper?
Or feel a patter on your shoe?
See how pale red ash
drifts like blossom:
little cinders of heart
on beds of stone.

This is a place, privileged.
A no-man's-land.
Each sheltering soul
a king -
kings in their own valley.

1995   *Patricia Foster*

ON THESE HILLS

On these hills
You trust no-one.

Certainly not the black dog
With his sabre snarl
Guarding the fitted kitchens
In restored farms;

Certainly not the farmhand
With his slippery sneer
Despising the hiker as intruder,
Amateur on the lambing pasture;

Certainly not the tractor driver
With his sullen scowl,
Steering a trailer of old loaves
Through steep ruts to the pig farm.

Trees remain leafless
In this upland April;
Only the hawthorn,
Beginning a green Easter
High above the crossed boughs,
Mitigates these crowns of thorns.

1995   *Martyn Halsall*

from: **OH, THE WILD, WILD MOORS**
   Blackstone Edge

My heart's away in the lonely hills,
Where I would gladly be -
On the rolling ridge of Blackstone Edge,
Where the wild wind whistles free!
There oft in careless youth I roved,
When summer days were fine;
And the meanest flower of the heathery waste
Delights this heart of mine!
Oh, the wild, wild moors; the wild, wild moors,
And the stormy hills so free;
Oh, the wild, wild moors; the wild, wild moors,
The sweet wild moors for me.

I fain would stroll on lofty Knowl,
And Rooley Moor again;
Or wildly stray one long bright day
In Turvin's bonny glens!
The thought of Wardle's breezy height
Fills all my heart with glee,
And the distant view of the hills so blue
Brings tears into my e'e!
Oh, the wild, wild moors; the wild, wild moors,
And the stormy hills so free;
Oh, the wild, wild moors; the wild, wild moors,
The sweet wild moors for me.

mid 19th century   *Edwin Waugh*

from
COME WHOAM TO THY CHILDER AN' ME

Aw've just mended th' fire wi' a cob;
Owd Swaddle has brought thi new shoon;
There's some nice bacon-collops o'th hob,
An' a quart o' ale posset i'th oon;
Aw've brought thi top-cwot, doesto know,
For th' rain's comin' deawn very dree;
An' th' har'stone's as white as new snow; -
Come whoam to thi childer an' me.

mid 19th C.   *Edwin Waugh*

WAUGH'S WELL
*High above the Dearden Valley is a spring,
where a bronze figurehead commemorates
the Lancashire poet, Edwin Waugh.*

Those features turn
to moorland green.
Words are water
welling up inside;

the cadence falls
to reservoirs
where the words
collect and glitter.

Text is landscape
printed with sheep,
green pages edged
with dry stone walls.

Materials come from
quarries of grit
and the workings
of water and wind.

Streams hold sky
and images of hills.
Utterance flows
or pauses in pools.

Liquid language
moves easily
through dialects
of bracken and gorse,

does not end
when the day does,
produces work
that is bound in stars.

1993　　*Chris Woods*

ON THE BLACKBURN ROAD TO BOLTON

On the Blackburn Road to Bolton,
Pay packet burning in pocket,
First hi-fi purchase in mind,
Passed a few shops, then stopped,
Amazed - eye-glazed - gob-smacked!
There it chose to stand, in rows
With the other ordinary shops,
On the Blackburn Road to Bolton
A cap shop; a window bursting,
With a pride of men's cloth caps.

There were blue caps, green caps,
'I'd rather not be seen' caps
Check caps, fleck caps,
'It goes well wi' me keks' caps.

There were red caps, dead caps,
'Wear on t' back o' head' caps,
Bright caps, night caps,
'Ready for the fight' caps,
Yob caps, bob caps,
'Right for any job' caps.

Creations from the past, persisting in the present,
In that window, on the Blackburn Road to Bolton.

1995   *Antoinette Loftus*

from
COME, MARY, LINK THI' ARM I' MINE

Eawr Tum has sent a bacon-flitch;
Eawr Jem a load o' coals;
Eawr Charlie's bought some pickters, an'
He's hanged 'em upo' th' wholes;
Owd Posy's white-weshed th' cottage through;
Eawr Matty's made it swet;
An Jack's gav me his Jarman flute
To play bi' th' fire at neet.

mid 19th C.   *Edwin Waugh*

CUTT WOOD, RISHTON

It is always there, living.
Across the lane, down the ditch, through the hedge.
Green breathing leaves,
acorns, tall grasses, spinning jennies.

> Cinder paths rough to unshod feet.
> Dark secret places.
> Spiders. frogs, unseen but felt and feared
> and killed from fear.

Canal, 'the cut', down Cutt Lane.
Dangerous, wet, fluid, sometimes frozen.
Don't go near! Forbidden land.
Death is fear and fear is death.

> Long hot, child-summers
> spent with freedom's joy, sun-ripened.
> Climbing trees, hard, rough, strong.
> Tempted higher, ever higher.
> Sitting on my branch flushed with exultation.

Bird's nest, don't touch!
Marble eggs, vulnerable, come to life
feather-covered, soft and warm.
Like baby's skin but not so smooth.

> Soon to quicken and be gone
> but not before they fill Cutt Wood
> with new-found voices.
> They, too, soar in exultation.

1995   *Valerie J. Calderwood*

HOGHTON TOWER

Witch country, this, of spell casting,
and poisoned land and iron spiked graves.
Yet the Tower's spirit is no wailing hag.

Her presence rustles where Minstrels played,
listens for muffled hooves
soft thudding her lover's approach.

Echo of the fatal shot chills air
as she passes; sighs anticipate
her cloistered chastity.

Fixed and forever he slides off his horse,
dies at her feet, elicits grief so potent
it moves dreams in minds unborn.

1995   *Alison Chisholm*

BAMBER BRIDGE

What's there to tell of Bamber Bridge,
This tarmac'd mile or so?
It's just a road from North to South.
To take the traffic flow.
You need not look in Domesday Book,
We are not mentioned there,
And in the lists of Heritage,
For us the page is bare.
We have no stately mansions
No pilgrims' holy well,
No famous choirs,
No soaring spires,
So what is there to tell?

We know that Romans used the road,
And Danes and Saxons too.
And the Roundheads, Scots, and British,
Have marched a mile or two,
But I think that the Americans,
Were the latest to pass through.

No, it's just an ordinary, unknown place,
Without a claim to fame,
And yet...and yet...in ancient days
Perhaps the dragons came?
And where their horny feet have trod,
Now lies this busy North-South road.
Alas! Without proof to suggest,
We will never know
If squamous, fiery dragons passed
This tarmac'd mile or so.

It's always been so peaceful here.
Please God, it always will.
So, what's to tell of Bamber Bridge?
What is there to tell?

Michael May

PLACE RHYME: *Pendle*

When Pendle wears its woolly cap
The farmers all may take a nap.

Trad

from: Iter Lancastrense

'Penigent, Pendle Hill, Ingleborough,
Three such hills be not all England through'.
I long to climbe up Pendle; Pendle stands
Rownd cop, survaijng all the wilde moore lands,
And Malkin toure, a little cottage, where
Reporte makes caitive witches meete to sweare
Their homage to the divell, and contrive
The deaths of men and beasts.

1636   *Richard James*

A LANCASHIRE WITCH

They may not burn me.
Although they light the faggots,
My flesh glow like molten metal
And my hair be a crown of points of pain,
My powers will put out the flames.

They may not swim me.
For I shall hang over flowing water
As a sad streaming willow
Or float as tangled reeds.
As I renounce my baptism
The water will reject me.

They may not hang me.
As they push me from the cart
I shall not dance from the beam
But fly as a black spiny bat.

I am all they said I was.
I have made a contract with the Devil,
Lain with him and bear his mark,
Suckled his familiar spirit
And given my blood, to have
All that I desired.

I sent my shape - foal,
Hare, black dog and toad -
To wither the udders of cattle,
Turn ale sour, milk to butter,
And cause young girls to fall sick
By making their pictures in clay.
With cunning men, wise women
Have I danced, following the old religion
Of cloven-footed spirits,
Horned God, Mother Goddess.

Let them take my store of herbs,
Bones and skin from the chimney place.
They never knew half my spells and charms,
But no minister can work them as well as I,
Who cannot say the Lord's Prayer.
I have no time for them,
Let them have their way. Well may they say:
'Her eyes are sunk in her head,
God bless us from her'.

1995　　　　　　　　　　　　*Mike Pattinson*

THE GYMNASTS

All at once I saw them
whirling arms and legs - the gymnasts
doing handstands on the high fell
linking past and future.
Here are the four winds caught
bridled and harnessed to our use.
Could Caratacos in his wild rides
have seen them! Now it seems
plans from another planet in our hands
are witnessed on Cold Clough Moor.
Tall and slim and white
twirling the air, they offer warmth and light
to thirty thousand living there below
in the rugged valley feathered with rowan and birch.
For them, no power-cuts or strikes
only the wind's variations.
But my first sight of the twenty-four
racing, while rooted, in unison
was wonder and delight electrified.

1995   *Phoebe Hesketh*

THE FOULRIDGE BLACKSMITH'S EPITAPH

from: The Annals of Colne

My sledge and hammer lie reclined
    My bellows too have lost their wind
My fire's extinct, my forge decayed
    Whilst in the dust my vice is laid
    My coals are spent, my iron is gone
My nails are drove, my work is done.

Anon

A BUILDER'S EPITAPH

My square's in a twist, my rule foreshorted
    My workshop is now long aborted.
My trowel's in rust, my hammer's at rest
    Tools that stood a thousand tests.
    I've used my mortar, I've used my sand
I'm in decay. My buildings stand.

1995   *Jack Whitaker*

from
WELCOME, BONNY BRID

Tha'rt welcome little bonny brid,
But shouldn't ha' come just when tha' did;
Toimes are bad.
We're short o' pobbies for eawr Joe,
But that, of course, tha didn't know,
Did ta, lad?...

But tho' we've childer two or three,
We'll mak' a bit o' reawm for thee,
Bless thee, lad!
Tha'rt th' prattiest brid we have i'th' nest,
So hutch up closer to mi breast;
Aw'm thi dad.

c 1861-5   *Samuel Laycock*

THE ROAD TO CHINGLE HALL

I leave the razzle of Blackpool
for the pastoral M55.

Always I notice the dead tree,
silhouetted signpost of the wind.
And the white house, tantalizing in its isolation;
and remember, through the travelling seasons,
the tang of the rape seed field in spring.

The Lancaster Canal, behind a hedge,
plays hide-and-seek.
Eight bridges pass
like bar-lines on a 4-line stave;
sheep nibble *grazissimo,*
            cattle munch *larghissimo.*
While all along the grass blows silver.

I take the exit to the Garstang road
where nasturtium verges still flicker in October;
turn right at the clustered crossroads
and accompany Broughton leaves choreographed by traffic;
acknowledge the side road to Beacon Fell
and purchase produce of free-running peckerland.

Down the lane on the right by the Goosnargh sign
I've half a mile of first gear bumps
where ghostly fog pirouetted a headlight welcome
on Hallowe'en.
I glance at the pond,
admire the floral choir, ranged by the farmhouse wall,
and the timeless steps...

1995   *Norah Mortimer*

CHINGLE HALL

No need for drawbridge now
to cross the threshold -
former papists' boundary to sanctuary -
the chapel free to view
where priests once hid.

So tourists come to History's secret diary
in the pocket of a Lancashire lane.

As selected pages turn,
part torn, part erased
or illegible with time,
they hear of soldier Utred -
recipient of this land in Harold's days -
who called himself De Singleton;
of his descendant, builder
of this lesser manor, moated,
thwarting enemies of fox and wolf.

They venerate the birth
and martyr's death of
Saint John Wall.
Enigma breathes.
Will Chingle Hall forever
draw its veil?

Sometimes a head will turn at a whiff of incense
or a glimpse of a monk at prayer,
of tragic Eleanor betrayed by...
or footsteps, an opened door, a latch alive.

Old inhabitants are here
reluctant to leave
their Lancashire lane.

1995   *Norah Mortimer*

PLACE RHYME

The Ribble, the Hodder, the Calder, the rain,
All flow into Mytton Demesne.

Trad

PLACE RHYME: *Ribchester*

'Tis written on a wall in Rome
Ribchester was rich as any town in Christendom.

Trad

IN SEARCH OF THE RIBBLE
(Alston Hall, 1991)

Out of the gate. Turn right.
Downhill between rimed hedgerows.
Tractors pass with odorous loads.
Danger - muck-spreaders at work.
Deceitful, forked-roads misdirect us.

Elusive footpaths skirt farmyards;
watchful collies bark a warning.
Penned, lowing cattle, coats ordure-matted,
regard us curiously.
Somewhere a bull roars frustration.

The pathway, hoof-rutted,
crackle-glazed by frost,
opens out beneath tall beeches
to the river -
wide, fast flowing, frozen-edged.

From bank to bank
wintry sunlight highlights ripples.
Wading bullocks
lapping the icy waters
make my teeth ache in sympathy.

1995   *Marie Murray*

THE TROUGH OF BOWLAND

The westward stream is shaded;
it sounds beneath a cloak of fir,
Scots pine, and the oaks
descended from the breadths
of ancient Bolland. Long since,
the Parkers earned their name
for keeping the King's Great Park.
The roe and the fallow herds
are gone; the white cattle, too,
called by music into Gisburn.

I am uneasy here: this loveliness
conceals some misery, seeped in
and running with the stream.
The feel of it survives the picnics
and the cars cramped into clearings
on its sunny days; by evening
they're gone: the valley's only
trees and water, the settled sheep
round a few stone houses threaded
by a pale road under moonlight
rippling with leaf-shadow.

But its lure is something morbid.
Again and again I go, alone
or safely befriended, probing
for what troubles me. Always
I leave it with relief: breathe
the expanse of the open moor -
where once I saw March hares
chasing in a wind-blown ring.

1995   *Pauline Keith*

BARN IN BOWLAND

The barn was built four hundred years ago.
It stands aside, its shoulder to the north
Wind, watching the wind turn tongues of brown grass.

Which is stronger: four centuries of stone,
Or wind, carrying a sheep's bleat on its back,
Crumbling the barrow-side with calloused hands?

You would not notice, but the wall gapes, 'Oh -'
Listen. Is that the wild cry of the wind
Or slow, a stone lament for centuries lost?

No one goes there. Except, sometimes, the rain.

1995   *Sara Monk*

PETER LAD: A SONG OF THE CROASDALE

In the morning, in the evening,
beyond sleep, beyond knowing,
above the roar of the river,
can you hear the voices calling,
Peter lad?

Mud-brown swollen water
snarls and froths
lace-white over the weir
where in summer warm
pools held idle trout.
Trees long past their prime
at length break from the bank
piecemeal. Great boughs
hold their twisted arms
above the torrent,
drowned patriarchs
caught in clefts of rock.

Peter lad, they call the pool
where the boy died
alone, long ago.
Were his calls drowned
by the winter weir's raging
or did the summer naiads
draw him to their lost land
below the river? Only the salmon,
silver gleaming upstream
or the heron, unbending in
his grey vigil, know...
and they will never tell.

In the morning, in the evening,
beyond sleep, beyond knowing,
above the roar of the river,
can you hear the voices calling,
Peter lad?

1995   *Averil King-Wilkinson*

RIBBLESDALE

Earth, sweet Earth, sweet landscape, with leaves throng
And louchèd low grass, heaven that dost appeal
To, with no tongue to plead, no heart to feel;
That canst but only be, but dost that long -

Thou canst but be, but that thou well dost; strong
Thy plea with him who dealt, nay does now deal,
Thy lovely dale down thus and thus bids reel
Thy river, and o'er gives all to rack or wrong.

And what is Earth's eye, tongue, or heart else, where
Else, but in dear and dogged man? - Ah, the heir
To his own selfbent so bound, so tied to his turn,
To thriftless reave both our rich round world bare
And none reck of world after, this bids wear
Earth brows of such care, care and dear concern.

1918 (written 1882)   *Gerard Manley Hopkins*

STONE DICTA

Walls which string the hills together,
fluent, articulate, smoothly syllabic;
they run rings around us, din our ears.

Brazen cheer-leaders of the long march
booming and chattering across the fells
they protect property, declare rights,
follow contours, determine ways.

Where rock is steep, walls cease
and conversation dies on the escarpment.
Above, they resume in a gabble of vowels,
apeing raw boulders, echoing scree.

At night they rattle in a car's headlights,
huddle closer to road margins,
undulate past in macintosh grey.

By torchlight on foot, they show new faces,
each stone ringing its own note.
At dawn they tail it over the horizon,
incantatory laughter in their wake.

1995   *Lauraine Palmeri*

DAY-SAVER TO PRESTON

Huddled houses in rough gardens
rubbish chucked over the fence
a nest of broken sheds

heavy stones in twists
of yellow polythene
hold sprawling haystacks down

two geese, a green Fishwick bus

licorice earth
beaten to a high ridged path
beside the Leyland Tyre and Rubber Company

a curving stream
like the burn of my childhood
leads to a sewage farm

a disused halt, gutted, grey
saplings breaking through the platform

white tips of pussy willow

1995   *Patricia Pogson*

PLACE RHYME: *Preston*

Proud Preston, poor people,
Low church, no steeple.

Trad

THE BALLAD OF PRESTON DOCK

Changes have happened on Preston Dock
Since the last ship left the town,
Warehouses, silos, petrol tanks gone,
Converted or else pulled down.

Shop for a week, buy burgers or cars,
Rent a fine office, so smart.
There's a cinema, homes and a public house -
Did ships once arrive and depart?

Ships came to town on the rising tide,
Riding the Ribble in from the sea,
Heavy with cargo, following lights
Leading surely to the quay.

'North' and 'South Sides' , and the large dock gates -
'Allsups' and 'Peddars', 'Marsh' and 'Main' -
Their names may soon be forgotten
But 'The Dock' will always remain.

Ships left the town on the tide,
Dropping down the Ribble from the quay,
Heavy with cargo, following lights
Leading outward to the sea.

'Ionic' and *'Doric'* sailed to Ireland
With cars and passengers too.
Scrap iron came, red-rusted from Spain,
Turin sent Fiats, brand new.

Once woodstacks, lorries and china clay,
White blocked wood pulp, edging the dock -
Now there's 'Texas', yachts and 'Morrisons' -
With a lighthouse - does it mock?

Changes have happened on Preston Dock
Since the last ship left the town:
New enterprise, full ahead, found the quay,
Relaunching proud Preston's renown.

1995   *Ted Harris*

RIBBLE ESTUARY

Once ships sailed past my window
bound for Preston on the tide,
small traders and the Irish Mail,
and cargo ships with cotton for the mills.
A busy port was Preston then,
but trade slackened and declined
and dredgers ceased to dredge.
Sand, mud and marram grass encroached,
and picnic tables sprouted on the Pilling turf
laid down by council men.

'Uncertain channels, much infernal mud
choked up with sand'.
A mariner's warning, written in a log
of long ago.
But still Peet's Light,
where Romans landed at Naze Point,
and Charlie's mast at Lytham,
ornamental on the Green.

Last ship that passage
to the sea to take,
'The Manxman' 1992,
towed down the channel
on the highest tide.
I watched her go, and linger
on a sandbank for a while,
almost as though reluctant to depart.

1995   *Betty Jones*

LIKE WINTER IN DELHI *(Lytham St Annes)*

Sand drifts one mile
says the sign that leads to
this sky blue, sand beige,
Accrington red brick
two-into-one town
that primly paddles its toes
in the Irish Sea.

Flat sands stretching out beneath
blue bowl sky upturned
invite kites and sandyachts
to catch the brisk winds
that gust forever in from the west,
blowing them home exhausted,
with their children and dogs.

Holiday flats, rest homes, pier,
fishermen's cottages, windmill
cluster along the banks
of the Ribble Estuary.

It's a long way to have come
from garden City flanked by the Jumna,
Lal Kila, crowded marketplaces,
scorching summers, drenching monsoon.
Rose rich winters when
wrapped in shawls we'd sit outside
shading our eyes from the sunlight.

Sometimes here, on a summer day
I shut my eyes, feeling the breeze
caress my face and hair.
It's like winter in Delhi.
It almost feels like home.

1995   *Seetha Shearer*

Lal Kila: Red Fort

LYTHAM ST ANNES

This corner of the world's at peace it seems
As Lytham sunlight drowns the afternoon,
Invading every fairway, bunker, green
And spilling over every grassy dune.
From here and there a distant glinting shaft
As irons are wielded silently and straight.
Green, Gary, Martin, John and I all laughed,
All holing out in ten or nine or eight.
Our four all running in - please overtake!
And while they did we'd sit and watch the planes,
Commanche shadows on the man-made lake,
Young pipers wasp-like dropping from their lanes.
In early summer haze we soldiered on
Till shadows of the afternoon grew long.

1988 *Mike Read*

from

THE FYLDE
A Song of Windmill Land

O, the Fylde's a bonny country, of flowery lane and lea,
With mountains on the morning side, and on the west the sea;
And a shining river winding through the Windmill Land between -
Farms, orchards, cornfields, villages, and woodland sweet and green.

late 19th C. *Allen Clarke*

FIRST SIGHTING

Where's the Tower?
Mum replies,
           You'll
See it soon,
Keep looking, chuck.

Dad says,
           Petrol
'll just last out
With luck.

But where?

Ahead.

But when?

- Don't keep pestering,
You'll see it when
You see it - then!

But Mum -

Do as your mother
Tells you, son.
Else I'll turn the
Car round. Don't
Start your sister off -

There; chuck, over
There. The Tower!
Look, everyone -

OOOOOOOO....

Takes summat to strike
The childer dumb...
Hey-ho, Blackpool, here we come!

1995   C. M. Coates

THE PLEASURE BEACH

The north-west coast stretches
from dock to dune to beach.
Along the gullied sands
the five piers pierce the sea.
Here, stone, sand and clay are whipped
into towering hotels, miles of promenades.
Cables and wires
lights for nights,
winding and winding for miles.

Above, the rides rise
on tiny tracks:
carts filled with heads -
from below just dots
at the top of the dippers;
each sampling snippet views
of coastline and Lancashire hills.

1995 *Ceri Courtenay*

BLACKPOOL (*In the Season*)

Brassy, ageless good time girl
Reclining on the sands
Flanked by both your sisters
Staid Cleveleys, prim St Annes

Salt spray crusts your painted face
Your perfumes stain the air
Hot dogs, chips and candy floss
Tossed beer cans in the square

Coarse, vulgar, friendly temptress
Seduction in your heart
Parting fools from common sense
And money is your art

Noisy, shouting, singing
No barriers of class
Accepting all, rejecting none
Laughing Lancashire lass

1995 *Sheila Clift*

LANDAU DRIVER

Clip clop clip clop up the Prom
Goes the landau driver Tom;
Sandy 'tache and sandy hair,
Brown cigar butt rooted there;
Ruddy face from sun and gale
And Mr Boddington's fine ale.
City Fathers make a fuss
'Landaus interfere w't' bus.
Get 'em cleared off Promenade,
Place is like a stable yard.'
But clip clop clip clop on goes Tom,
Sand grown man on sand grown Prom.
Crack!
Stand back!
Burst tyre!
Back fire!
Away at a gallop the horse in a fright
Scatters the people to left and to right,
Faster and faster past this pier and that,
Tom grasps the reins with a hand on his hat.
Tom's in control
At the Metropole;
And clip clop clip, he takes his fare
To Red Bank Road via Cocker Square.

Along the Prom it's said
Tom's dead.
Black horse, black plumes, black coach take Tom where
                                             he will lie
In Blackpool earth, beneath a Blackpool sky.
Twice twenty landaus walk behind from Common Edge
                                          to Robins Lane,
You'll never see the like of it again.
Sad...Grand lad!
But clip clop clip clop up the Prom
Trots young Tommy, son of Tom.

1995   *Nancy Clare Wynne*

LAST NIGHT

Hanging above our heads
garish tea-pots pour
glitter into sparkling cups.
Miss Muffet sits - but runs
repeatedly from that spider.

Humpty Dumpty falls
four times in one minute;
kings and queens and teddy bears
dance along the prom, while
from the Tower a laser scrawls the sky.

On this last Sunday evening
everything is open:
windows, funfairs, pubs, sex-shops,
mouths for chips, candyfloss and pop-corn;
coaches and hotels spill people out.

As dawn breaks, a bossy wind
chases debris into corners
and the sea sweeps in
to impose order on
this razzmatazz of a town.

1994   **Peggy Poole**

BLACKPOOL WIND

A gale that rakes the sea and lifts
Its breakers up to Bispham cliffs
While wooden slatted piers vibrate
Along the coast to Squires Gate

Savage blasts that snatch the rain
To fling against the tramcar pane
In foaming droplets like the spray
That honeycombs the rocks away

A force that hammers stinging skin
And moulds it round the bones within
That drowns the sounds of fruit machines
Along the Golden Mile of dreams

Thrusting gusts of grit-filled air
That scour the roofs of Talbot Square
And make the grudging iron tower
Bend its head to nature's power

1995   *Sheila Clift*

DANCING IN THE DARK - BLACKPOOL

To the Tower Ballroom without a partner,
dancing alone, but recalling each pulse.
Less irksome than to shunt an unfamiliar
dodgy hip around the polished floor.
One flesh, oblivious to the idle glance,
he floats across the room,
coming here often to renew promises.
Unable now to sit one out with tired feet
or escape to the bar, perhaps to lose
the fading beat, the time he's keeping.
Up through the floor the console rises.
Lights.   Music.   Curtains.

I smile and push my partner into
a reluctant rumba.   Two basics,
then pretend to stamp on cockroaches.
Never do anything on the 1 beat unless
it's to slide with style into the side step.
Hold her tenderly, pretend to be in love.

1995   *Michael Cunningham*

from
THE VIEW FROM THE GALLERY
(Grand Theatre, Church Street, Blackpool)

Perched in my red plush magpie nest
High above the limelit square of stage,
Clouds of music billowing upwards,
Showering enchanted notes like rain.
Forgotten grime and flaking gilt
Are lost in deep dramatic shadow.
Secure in this shabby paradise,
I watch the shifting coloured shapes,
Kaleidoscoped and jewel bright,
Flit in the light like rainbow moths.
This place is aptly called the gods,
For here we catch the very breath of heaven.
Here sit the penniless disciples
Of the gods of beauty: students,
Neophytes, sacrificing on this altar
Roast beef or new shoes
To buy some magic.
A gathering crescendo lifts us on its swell
And applause breaks like a crashing wave
On a storm-torn Northern beach....

1995   *Jennifer Smethurst*

BLEAK WYRE

A cold and brave February surfer
Surfs the wind across Fleetwood's trachea,
Its bleak estuary. The moon calls its slave
To ebb and leaves a wet ribbed sandy architrave
Around barnacled boulders and stranded flotsam.
Nylon rope ends, beer bottles, old oakum
Fish crates, plastic and wood - jettisoned,
Flotsamed, abandoned. Life's end.

A dead boat's rib cage
Climbs out of the mud giving multistage
Territory for gulls and starlings,
Food haunts for dunlins and lapwings.
The sun shivers away for southern
Climes, the wind increases, the tern
Sails seaward and the surfer retreats;
But the dunlin still probes and eats.

1995   *Roger Chamberlain*

SUNDERLAND POINT   (LUNE ESTUARY)
Epitaph on Sambo, a Negro Servant, died 1763

Full sixty years the angry Winter's Wave
Has thundering dashed this bleak and barren Shore,
Since Sambo's Head laid in this lonely Grave
Lies still and ne'er will hear their turmoil more.

Full many a Sandbird chirps upon the Sod
And many a Moonlight Elfin round him trips,
Full many a Summer Sunbeam warms the Clod
And many a teeming Cloud upon him drips.

But still he sleeps - till the awakening Sounds
Of the Archangel's Trump new life impart,
Then the Great Judge His Approbation founds
Not on Man's Colour but his Worth of Heart.

1796   *James Watson*

from: **SUNDERLAND POINT AND RIBCHESTER**

Sunderland Point, where sea, wind, sky
Dispute dominion, on a spur of land
So bitter that you'd think no one would take
The trouble to go there.
                    Here SAMBO lies,
A faithful NEGRO, who (attending his Mafter
From the Weft Indies) DIED
On his Arrival at Sunderland.

It is, of course, unconsecrated ground.

Now children stagger here on pilgrimage,
Their offerings the sort of things you'd find
On a pet's grave: a cross of driftwood, lashed
With binder-twine; a Woolworth vase,
Chocked up with grit and pebbles, crammed
With dead wild flowers.
                    Sam lies very low.
You can allow him any voice you like.
Despair, pneumonia, exile, love, are variously
Thought to have killed him. A good place
To bring the kids in summer at weekends....

1987   *U.A. Fanthorpe*

VIEW FROM THE LUNE AQUEDUCT, SEPTEMBER

Weeds where rope was taut,
massive arches span,
bear weight of neglected canal.
A sunny towpath stroll
on a Sunday afternoon.

Lean on the parapet, watch fishermen
spin for sea-trout far below.
Their dogged patience as they cast
mirrored in this monument
to man's ingenuity.

>   A view worth the climb.
>   A time for gongoozling,
>   water-weeds sway
>   above and below.
>   Subdued, the traffic growls.

Into this well of calm, a raucous din:
a jaunty barge of trippers nears.
We exchange stares, smiles, waves;
they putter by, recede.
Somnolence seeps back again.

1995   Averil King-Wilkinson

SEEING THROUGH LANCASTER CASTLE

Topping her hillock this dual purpose queen
with polished locks, corners an estuary's open sky
to oversee the silted Lune which slavers
and swallows at its appointed tide regardless

of appetite. Short stay tourists park around
her grassy skirt, a moat of fenders winking
at the twenty-minute sign. Bear left for guidance:
far right inclines to incarceration.

This castle sprawls firm. Its function still: full
complement of prisoners, courtroom ringing
with living retribution. Plus Heritage
Centre. Apt, for kinsfolk queue through

centuries at the great arched door, subdued
and child-accompanied, drawing ever-nearer their
free entry, yearning for real life ghosts
who materialise on weekend afternoons.

Adjoining lodging houses offer luncheon
for avenging legal angels who chew
too long, caressing cases of handless
corpses and claret, reminiscing...

Thirty years ago, a witch's tongue almost
twitched in its mounting, on my school visit here.
That wizened leather, without taste, has been removed -
for the second time. Still on tap, though, is

a fine 'hands-off' experience. Be banged up
in dungeon pitch, 'Just to get the flavour'. Taste
dark, touch emptiness, feel eternity.
And, with widening eyes, see. See it all.

1995   *Joyce Knowles*

S. MARTIN'S COLLEGE, LANCASTER
(for Robert Clayton)

Sword into felt-tip, Mars into Martin
The Oxfam saint. It's true about plough-shares:
Almost anything warlike, kept long enough,

Rusts into use. Armoury was where library is,
Since books are dangerous as bayonets,
And keep their point longer. Where officers

And gentlemen once toasted *The King the Duke,*
Bragged about whores and horses, the soft
Uncritical hum of the photocopier, plans

For peaceful teaching practice manoevres
In Morecambe. Inside the compound the urgent
Dilatory promenade of study, irregular presence

Of willow and flowering crab, where other ranks
Stamped their exact angles, angled their eyes
As the sergeant told them. Gone, all gone.

Now on the barrack square the chapel's shaft,
Collecting eyes like an after-dinner hostess,
Suggests a move elsewhere; in the keep now

TV's inhuman eye invigilates. Only the dumb
Dangling ghost of the suicidal batman
Still persists, and the guard-room dogs,

Nab de Cordova and Bob, unfailing garrison,
In their regimental graves, in the old tradition.
Two chiselled Lancashire roses. No flag; not a drum.

1987 *U.A. Fanthorpe*

TIME FOR BED

Off duty at 4.15 p.m.
Just time to change, then
you, waiting for me
in your car, face
glowed by the setting sun.
Rush-hour along the river road
from Lancaster to Morecambe
where we would buy
a bed
big bed, big bed
to share with you, beloved,
such tides between us
and we talked and talked.
In the slow-moving traffic
two cars ahead,
a clumsy fat boy of eight or so
running across, was winged
like a bird. He tried to fly,
rose, then fell again.
He lay on the road, and I,
warm with your love, and
anticipation of the bed
knelt beside him,
held his head
on my lap, while you
directed the lorries past us.
Their wheels, higher
than my head, turned cautiously
past the bird and me -
slivers of trust stretched
between all three of us.
From the pavement his mother watched,
as wheels rolled over my blue-
and-white long skirt -
I have it still,
never threw it away.
Ambulancemen, who through the day
swapped ribald jokes with me,
showed no recognition; no uniform,
long skirt disguising me.
Into the car again,
and the bed, bought in haste
(never comfortable),
hard, unrelenting memorial.

1995   *Anne Spillard*

THE PROMENADE, MORECAMBE, OFF SEASON

A forbidden, rickety pier
sporting torn posters of Big Daddy.

Scarred dinghies swashing at anchor.
Wingless gulls tucked in themselves.

Above the rain-measly esplanade
guests' faces, white flags at windows.

A haunch-splayed Alsatian retching,
brought to heel by a snorted leash.

A boardsailor half a mile out,
capsizing his image, heaving up again.

Takeaway trays choking a litter bin.
A varicose waitress trashing her fag.

Waves grey as limp mortar
mooching in regardless, slopped back.

1991   *Geoffrey Holloway*

MORECAMBE BAY

Our feet crush the coracles of shells;
Mud-flats deepen from the sea-wall,
Planed by a tide's dragging brown blade.
Oyster-catchers spoon shingle, the grey
Ash of knot and sanderling flakes up
Into sky crackling with their cries
And joint-racking cold.

An old man watches wintering curlew:
His overcoat is tied with string,
His dog investigates a scummy tide-mark.
A couple walk hand in hand at the sea's edge:
Sun warps their shadows onto sand, wind
Nudges them towards the feeding birds.

A fishing boat slowly trawls the lamination
Of light upon water;
Our feet soak in limpet-struck pools,
Your scarf streams scarlet from dark tangles
Of hair that tonight will taste of salt.

The cranes at Barrow-in-Furness break
The skyline with iron exclamations,
Rivers lug their silt out to a sea
Weighted with excrement and isotopes.

Wind x-rays our hands, the bones
Show clean as fillets.
Mud sucks at our feet, lets go, sucks, sucks.

1989   *Graham Mort*

NIGHT SHRIMPING (*Morecambe Bay*)

Moon's out un tide's up
We're off wi' Joe o'er Lune
Tu tek 'er quiet ower sand
After wee lile shrimp.

Off from dock and down tu point
Watter lappin' side ut boat,
Tekkin it quietly ower sand
After bonny fish un shrimp.

Taxi engine boomin' loud,
Pole ower side, feelin' way,
Tekkin it quietly ower sand
After scavenger shrimp.

Cockerham leet comin' wi' bar,
'We're grounded ! Ower side un push!'
Pushin' it ower sand,
Witched fut sake o' shrimp.

Nets out un warps taut,
Fire's burnin' breet int' stove,
Heatin't watter out o' sea
Fut boilin' o' shrimp.

Tide's turnin', fish box full,
Whoam and sell ower catch,
Twelve hours leep un off again,
After wee lile shrimp.

1980   **Mike Cooper**

STRANGE IMAGE AT WARTON CRAG

At the summit of the steps
we sit in strong sunlight, talk
of magic while Spring
continues her struggle among
pavements of limestone.
Like a pricking of blood
we worry how Edwardian
women came here to clamber
down sheer sides, standing poised
for a camera lens,
long skirted, with parasols
making their composure as odd
as narrow stairways hewn in rock.
We angle the photograph
trying to fathom
unruffled blouses and hats.

1995   *Cynthia Kitchen*

CAVE REVISITED, SILVERDALE 1990
(For Paul)

Aged four or thereabouts, I came, called
by you to see this cave. And did I climb
the six feet to the mouth and venture,

not too far, the inner dark? Today
I saw it half a mile away and knew:
reminder of some distant thing from mind's

deep space. Now, some fifty one years on,
drawn near, I recognize my archetypal cave,
the cave my mind conceives at every mention

of the word, not knowing why till now. Why,
seeing it again, do I remember this about
the place and nothing more? A doorway

to the womb perhaps, or entrance to some
deeper mystery, which awed and called me then,
and still has power to draw me to myself

here: where light confronts the dark,
the present moment fused into the past
with you, blending future meanings

too cavernous, by far, to be defined.

1995   *Alan Gaunt*

NEW YEAR'S EVE, 1913: CARTMEL PRIORY

O, Cartmel bells ring soft to-night,
   And Cartmel bells ring clear;
But I lie far away tonight,
   Listening with my dear;

Listening in a frosty land
   Where all the bells are still
And the small-windowed bell-towers stand
   Dark under heath and hill.

I thought that, with each dying year,
   As long as life should last,
The bells of Cartmel I should hear
   Ring out an aged past:

The plunging, mingling sounds increase
   Darkness's depth and height,
The hollow valley gains more peace
   And ancientness tonight:

The loveliness, the fruitfulness,
   The power of life lived there
Return, revive, more closely press
   Upon that midnight air.

But many deaths have place in men
   Before they come to die;
Joys must be used and spent, and then
   Abandoned and passed by.

Earth is not ours; no cherished space
   Can hold us from life's flow,
That bears us thither and thence by ways
   We knew not we should go.

O, Cartmel bells ring loud, ring clear,
   Through midnight deep and hoar,
A year new-born, and I shall hear
   The Cartmel bells no more.

1925   *Gordon Bottomley*

THE LEVENS ESTUARY (ULVERSTON SANDS)
from: The Prelude, Book 10

...Over the smooth sands
Of Leven's ample estuary lay
My journey, and beneath a genial sun,
With distant prospect among gleams of sky
And clouds, and intermingling mountain-tops,
In one inseparable glory clad...

As I advanced, all that I saw or felt
Was gentleness and peace. Upon a small
And rocky island near, a fragment stood
(Itself like a sea rock) the low remains
(With shells encrusted, dark with briny weeds)
Of a dilapidated structure, once
A Romish chapel, where the vested priest
Said matins at the hour that suited those
Who crossed the sands with ebb of morning tide.
Not far from that still ruin all the plain
Lay spotted with a variegated crowd
Of vehicles and travellers, horse and foot,
Wading beneath the conduct of their guide
In loose procession through the shallow stream
Of inland waters; the great sea meanwhile
Heaved at safe distance, far retired...

      I pursued my way
Along that very shore which I had skimmed
In former days, when - spurring from the Vale
Of Nightshade, and St Mary's mouldering fane,
And the stone abbot, after circuit made
In wantonness of heart, a joyous band
Of schoolboys hastening to their distant home
Along the margin of the moonlight sea -
We beat with thundering hoofs the level sand.

1850 (written by 1805)   *William Wordsworth*

THE TOWER ON THE HOAD, ULVERSTON

Look from thy tower - strong wish we mortals have
That deeds should be remembered after death -
Look forth, and tell the listening lands beneath,
From torchy Furness to the charnel cave
Of Heysham's cliff, that since the Leven's wave,
With confluent Craik, at tide-time held its breath
And halted up the vale, no surer wreath
Than duty honoured can outlive the grave!
If hence no rosy star at sunset gleam,
To guide the keel that beats from shoal to shoal,
And cheer the sailor on his lonely road,
White as thy tower, high-lifted, still must beam
The lamp that lit thee, Barrow, to thy goal,
A nation's honour on thy native Hoad.

1887　　　　　　　　　*H.D. Rawnsley*

ST. CUTHBERT'S CHURCH, ALDINGHAM

O'er northern mountain, marsh and moor,
From sea to sea, from shore to shore,
Seven years St. Cuthbert's corpse they bore...

　　　　　　　　　Old Rhyme

FURNESS ABBEY

Here would the aged pilgrim gladly stay
To rest him in these hospitable halls;
Here where the night disconsolately falls
With song and story keep the night at bay.
Here did the shadowy brethren, white and grey,
Move to and fro within their stately walls,
And bind and loose the burdens of their thralls
Nor ever from the poor man turn away.
Alas! within the Abbot's painted room
Rich with armorial rose and Eastern palms,
The ferns are growing and the harebells bloom,
And blackberry for all who ask an alms,
Where, through the vale of nightshade in the gloom,
The screech owl hoots his penitential psalms.

1907   *Mary Coleridge*

from: **UNDER THE HORIZON**
   (Barrow-in-Furness)

Great ships had moored against the western hills
(beyond Scarbarrow, Yarlside and The Billings)
their derricks, masts and funnels
irritating the skyline, capturing early sun,
a stark jawline of silhouettes by evening.

Great ships, moored against the western hills...
All through childhood it seemed to me
that Barrow's landmarks were about to sail
down Walney Channel to the Irish Sea.
The smokestacks of a liner, hull-down,

were Roosecote's power-station chimneys;
her deck-hoists, pylons; the shipyard's scaffolding
of cranes filling holds with stone, potatoes,
timber, iron ore; unloading
grain from Canada, cane sugar from Tobago...

For thirty years I kept my distance, my illusions.
Always the intervening fields, ploughed black and red.
On higher ground, I cultivated visions
of a better world, almost destroyed
when my time came to go under the horizon.

1995   *Robert Drake*

ON DUDDON MARSH

This is the shore, the line dividing
The dry land from the waters, Europe
From the Atlantic; this is the mark
That God laid down on the third day.
Twice a year the high tide sliding,
Unwrapping like a roll of oil-cloth, reaches
The curb of the mud, leaving a dark
Swipe of grease, a scaled-out hay

Of wrack and grass and gutterweed. Then
For full three hundred tides the bare
Turf is unwatered except for rain;
Blown wool is dry as baccy; tins
Glint in the sedge with not a sight of man
For two miles round to drop them there.
But once in spring and once again
In autumn, here's where the sea begins.

1954   *Norman Nicholson*

BLACK COMBE
(from Broughton-in-Furness)

Far off, and half revealed, 'mid shade and light,
Blackcomb half smiles, half frowns; his mighty form
Scarce bending in to peace;- more formed to fight
A thousand years of struggles with a storm
Than bask one hour, subdued by sunshine warm
To bright and breezeless rest; yet even *his* height
Towers not o'er this world's sympathies; he smiles,
While many a human heart to pleasure's wiles
Can bear to bend, and still forget to rise;
As though he, huge and heath-clad, on our sight,
Again rejoices in his stormy skies,
Man loses vigour in unstable joys.
Thus tempests find Blackcomb invincible,
While we are lost, who should know life so well!

1845 (written 1840)   *Branwell Bronte*
first published in The Yorkshire Gazette, May 1845

from: **THE CHARCOAL BURNERS**
(High Furness, where charcoal was manufactured;
Low Furness, where it was used in smelting iron ore
from the mines)

Soon after dawn the men and carts arrive
and horses, fresh uncreaked from night's sleep,
stand sorrow-eyed within the wood.
The charcoal pit lies derelict and deep in fern;
the burners' hut a sagging den; and piles of wood,
stacked months before, overgrown in tangled grass
seeming waste, but by those woodmen known and understood....

All night and all next day the charcoal men
nurse the smouldering mound,
pouring earth on spurts of flame,
splashing water from the beck,
damping flames and snatching sleep
as best they may, on bracken-beds and turf....

Slowly, the cooled mound is turned back.
The tired burners smile. The prize, the charcoal,
glistens satin-black, and rings clear as a bell.

mid 20th C. *Irvine Hunt*

from: **THE VETERANS**

They were the natural climbers
Working in the grain of the rock,
Short men with hefty calves and precise hands,
Small enough for me to identify with,
Old enough to be the kind of brother
Who tunnels through to manhood maybe a decade
Before oneself, grows hair in the crutch
And bloodies the knuckles half a generation
Before I learned not to blush, before
I left Kincorth behind me and the horizon
Of my world moved southwards
Nearly as far as Watford.

Two Norths count for me:
North of the Mounth, where the Wells of Dee,
invisibly translucent, send their impulse
Through seventy miles of granite to the sea;
North of the Ribble, where the monochrome
Of Cumbria's hay and pasture fields
Is gentle enough to make me call it 'home'....

1987   *David Craig*

CLIMBING FOR BIRDS'-EGGS
from: The Prelude, Book 1

... In the high places, on the lonesome peaks
Where'er, among the mountains and the winds,
The Mother Bird had built her lodge. Though mean
My object and inglorious, yet the end
Was not ignoble. Oh! when I have hung
Above the raven's nest, by knots of grass
And half-inch fissures in the slippery rock
But ill sustain'd, and almost, as it seem'd
Suspended by the blast which blew amain,
Shouldering the naked crag...
            ... at that time
While on the perilous ridge I hung alone,
With what strange utterance did the loud dry wind
Blow through my ears! the sky seem'd not a sky
of earth, and with what motion mov'd the clouds!

1850 (written by 1805)   William Wordsworth

David Craig notes that this is 'the first piece of climbing literature in English' **(Native Stones, 1987)**

THE THUNDERSTORM

When Coniston Old Man was younger
And his deep-quarried sides were stronger,
Goats may have leaped about Goat's Water;
But why the tarn that looks like its young daughter
Though lying high under the fell
Should be called Blind Tarn, who can tell?

Far from Dow Crag, passing it by,
I saw it as a dark presageful eye;
And soon I knew that I was not mistaken
Hearing the thunder the loose echoes waken
About Scafell and Scafell Pike
And feeling the slant raindrops strike.

And when I came to Walna Pass
Hailstones hissing and hopping among the grass,
Beneath a rock I found a hole;
But with sharp crack and rumbling roll on roll
So quick the lightning came and went
The solid rock was like a lighted tent.

1936   *Andrew Young*

CONISTON WATER
from: Iteriad or Three Weeks Among The Lakes

...When dinner was over, as still it did rain,
We thought that we scarcely need longer remain:
So, ordered the carriage, and with no good will,
We ordered that pest of all travels - the bill.
May the money bear witness how quickly they made it.
 - Much quicker than we were inclined to have paid it!
Though, without further grumbling, the silver we gave,
And gallopped away from old Coniston's wave.
Yet, ere we should leave it in tempest and rain,
We, turning, looked back on its waters again.
With its deep-bosomed billows in front lay the lake,
Whose waters divided by mountain and cape,
All open and bare they, full lonely did lie,
Exposing their breast to the shadowy sky:
Retiring in distance they mistily lay;
And fainter each inlet, and softer each bay;
Till, appearing no more, by the wild tempest tost,
'Mid mountains and clouds in the distance were lost.
Those mountains, all mistily softened away,
Appeared like thin clouds at the dawn of a day;
Still darker and deeper, in bolder relief,
As, nearer approaching, and rising the chief,
The mighty Old Man, with his dark summit reft
Nearer and sterner arose on our left.
Oh, such was the view, sir, and we very well did
Look over each spot as we amply beheld it,
Then turned and rode off...

1830   *John Ruskin (aged 11)*

RUSKIN AT REST
Brantwood, Sunday, January 21st, 1900

The Rose of morning fades, and ghostly pale
The mountains seem to move into the rain,
The leafless hedges sigh, the water-plain
Sobs, and a sound of tears is in the Vale;
For he whose spirit-voice shall never fail,
Whose soul's arm ne'er shall lifted be in vain -
God's Knight, at rest beyond the touch of pain
Lies clad in Death's impenetrable mail.

And all the men whose helmets ever wore
The wild red-rose St George for sign has given
Stand round, and bow the head and feel their swords,
And swear by him who taught them deeds not words
To fight for Love, till, as in days of yore
Labour have joy, and earth be filled with Heaven.

1906   *H.D. Rawnsley*

TO HAWKSHEAD ACROSS WINDERMERE
from: The Prelude, Book 4

I bounded down the hill shouting amain
For the old Ferryman; to the shout the rocks
Replied, and when the Charon of the flood
Had staid his oars, and touched the jutting pier,
I did not step into the well-known boat
Without a cordial greeting. Thence with speed
Up the familiar hill I took my way
Towards that sweet Valley where I had been reared;
'Twas but a short hour's walk, ere veering round
I saw the snow-white church upon her hill
Sit like a throned Lady, sending out
A gracious look all over her domain.
Yon azure smoke betrays the lurking town;
With eager footsteps I advance and reach
The cottage threshold where my journey closed.

1850 (written by 1805)   William Wordsworth

CAROL

There was a Boy bedded in bracken,
Like to a sleeping snake all curled he lay;
On his thin navel turned this spinning sphere,
Each feeble finger fetched seven suns away.
He was not dropped in good-for-lambing weather,
He took no suck when shook buds sing together,
But he is come in cold-as-workhouse weather,
      Poor as a Salford child.

c.1936   *John Short*

SKATING ON ESTHWAITE WATER
from: The Prelude, Book 1

And in the frosty season, when the sun
Was set, and visible for many a mile
The cottage windows blazed through twilight gloom,
I heeded not their summons: happy time
It was indeed for all of us - for me
It was a time of rapture! Clear and loud
The village clock tolled six, - I wheeled about,
Proud and exulting like an untired horse
That cares not for his home. All shod with steel,
We hissed along the polished ice in games
Confederate, initiative of the chase
And woodland pleasures, - the resounding horn,
The pack loud chiming, and the hunted hare.
So through the darkness and the cold we flew,
And not a voice was idle; with the din
Smitten, the precipices rang aloud;

The leafless trees and every icy crag
Tinkled like iron; while far distant hills
Into the tumult sent an alien sound
Of melancholy not unnoticed, while the stars
Eastward were sparkling clear, and in the west
The orange sky of evening died away.
Not seldom from the uproar I retired
Into a silent bay, or sportively
Glanced sideways, leaving the tumultuous throng,
To cut across the reflex of a star
That fled, and flying, still before me gleamed
Upon the grassy plain; and oftentimes,
When we had given our bodies to the wind,
And all the shadowy banks on either side
Came sweeping through the darkness, spinning still
The rapid line of motion, then at once
Have I, reclining back upon my heels,
Stopped short; yet still the solitary cliffs
Wheeled by me - even as if the earth had rolled
With visible motion her diurnal round!
Behind me did they stretch in solemn train,
Feebler and feebler, and I stood and watched
Till all was tranquil as a dreamless sleep.

1850 (written by 1805)   **William Wordsworth**

DEAR NATIVE REGIONS
written in anticipation of leaving school at Hawkshead

Dear native regions, I foretell,
From what I feel at this farewell,
That, whereso'er my steps may tend,
And whenso'er my course shall end,
If in that hour a single tie
Survive of local sympathy,
My soul will cast the backward view,
The longing look alone on you.

Thus, while the Sun sinks down to rest
Far in the regions of the west,
Though to the vale no parting beam
Be given, not one memorial gleam,
A lingering light he fondly throws
On the dear hills where first he rose

William Wordsworth (aged 16)

INDEX OF POETS

Anon, 10, 22, 30, 31, 42, 43
Ashbrook, John, 41
Baldock, Carole, 33, 51
Bardsley, Wendy, 49
Bottomley, Gordon, 99
Brett, Mary, 45
Bronte, Branwell, 104
Byrom, John, 43
Calderwood, Valerie J., 63
Calvert, John, 27, 38
Cassidy, John, 15
Chappell, Arthur, 44
Chamberlain, Roger, 88
Chisholm, Alison, 64
Clarke, Allen, 82
Cleary, Lance, 38
Clift, Sheila, 34, 84, 87
Coates, C.M., 83
Coleridge, Mary, 102
Coles, Gladys Mary, 20, 23
Cooper, Mike, 96
Courtenay, Ceri, 84
Craig, David, 106
Craven, Ken, 50
Cunningham, Michael, 87
Daunt, Will, 19
Doherty, Alan, 17
Drake, Robert, 103
Drayton, Michael, 12
England, Gerald, 41, 47
Fanthorpe, U.A., 89, 92
Fitchett, John, 30
Foster, Patricia, 58
Gaunt, Alan, 98
Geras, Adele, 49
Gerrard, Sue, 28, 32

Hall, Bessie, 53
Halsall, Martyn, 59
Harris, Ted, 79
Henri, Adrian, 56
Hesketh, Phoebe, 9, 52, 68
Holloway, Geoffrey, 94
Holroyd, Eileen, 39
Hopkins, Gerard Manley, 76
Horrocks, Barbara, 54
Hunt, Irvine, 105
Jackson, Rev., 54
James, Richard, 66
Johnston, Kathleen, 50
Jones, Betty, 24, 80
Keith, Pauline, 73
King-Wilkinson, Averil, 75, 90
Kitchen, Cynthia, 97
Knowles, Joyce, 91
Laycock, Samuel, 69
Loftus, Antoinette, 62
MacDermott, Tony, 13
McGough Roger, 26
McGovern, Peter, 26
Mallinson, J. David, 46, 48
Masefield, John, 22
May, Michael, 12, 65
Mellors, W.A., 39
Mitchell, Brian, 57
Monk, Sara, 74
Morgan, Albert, 29, 35
Mort, Graham, 16, 95
Mortimer, Norah, 70, 71
Murray, Marie, 72
Nagle, Frances, 18
Nicholson, Norman, 104
Palmeri, Lauraine, 77

Pattinson, Mike, 67
Perry, George, 21
Pogson, Patricia, 78
Poole, Peggy, 86
Prince, John Critchley, 11
Rawnsley, H.D., 101, 109
Read, Mike, 82
Roscoe, William, 21
Ross, Margaret, 27
R.S.K., 43
Ruskin, John, 108
Schiller, Daphne, 38
Shearer, Seetha, 81
Short, John, 110
Simpson, Matt, 24
Smethurst, Jennifer, 88
Smith, Deirdre Armes, 40
Spillard, Anne, 93
Stanbury, Jean, 11
Street, Peter, 36
Thompson, Francis, 41
Topping, Angela, 37
Trad, 21, 30, 66, 72, 78
Wake, Brian, 25
Ward, John, 14, 44
Watson, James, 89
Waugh, Edwin, 60, 62
Whitaker, Jack, 69
Woodcock, Deirdre, 55
Woodcock, Margaret, 52
Woods, Chris, 56, 61
Wordsworth, William, 100, 106, 109, 110, 111
Wynne, Nancy Clare, 85
Young, Andrew, 18